T0300249

Routledge Revivals

Managing the British Economy

First published in 1968 *Managing the British Economy* attempts to trace the development of what has passed for economic planning in Britain in the 1960's and, at the same time, to observe the activities of those engaged in the operation and the effect of their actions on business and industry. In writing this book, the author has had in mind the difficulties of businessmen in keeping track of 'who does what' in the Economy. Experience in industry and in the field of management education has shown him that managers often have difficulties in placing their own operations in the national context and he attempts here to help the reader understand how the system works in practice. How do the new arrangements tie in with the old? How does any government influence the running of the economy? What kind of system are we moving towards?

This is a must read for scholars and researchers of British economy and economic history of Britain.

Managing the British Economy

A guide to economic planning in Britain since 1962

Richard Bailey

Routledge
Taylor & Francis Group

First published in 1968
by Hutchinson & Co.

This edition first published in 2023 by Routledge
4 Park Square, Milton Park, Abingdon, Oxon, OX14 4RN

and by Routledge
605 Third Avenue, New York, NY 10017

Routledge is an imprint of the Taylor & Francis Group, an informa business

Publisher's Note
The publisher has gone to great lengths to ensure the quality of this reprint but points out that some imperfections in the original copies may be apparent.

Disclaimer
The publisher has made every effort to trace copyright holders and welcomes correspondence from those they have been unable to contact.

A Library of Congress record exists under ISBN: 0090881001

ISBN: 978-1-032-50934-1 (hbk)
ISBN: 978-1-003-40033-2 (ebk)
ISBN: 978-1-032-50936-5 (pbk)

Book DOI 10.4324/9781003400332

Managing the British Economy

A guide to economic planning
in Britain since 1962

RICHARD BAILEY

HUTCHINSON OF LONDON

HUTCHINSON & CO (*Publishers*) LTD
178–202 Great Portland Street, London W1

London Melbourne Sydney
Auckland Bombay Toronto
Johannesburg New York

First published 1968

*This book has been set in Baskerville, printed in Great Britain
on Antique Wove paper by Anchor Press, and
bound by Wm. Brendon, both of Tiptree, Essex*

09 088100 1

Contents

For Hilda

Preface

This book is an attempt to explain the operation of the machinery by which the British economy is managed. It was written after a period of secondment to the National Economic Development Office, which was divided into two almost equal halves by the 1964 General Election. I have not set out to analyse the development of the economy in the 1960s except in so far as this was necessary to explain the purpose of the different Ministries or Government agencies now in being. However, as much of the present machinery of government has been adapted or improvised to meet changes in economic conditions both at home and abroad, some of these have inevitably forced their way into the foreground.

I should like to express my gratitude to various individuals and organisations for encouragement, help and advice, and particularly to Miss Joan Wimble for typing the drafts.

RICHARD BAILEY

Introduction

The idea of writing this book arose out of experience in lecturing to businessmen at Ashridge Management College and elsewhere on the running of the economy. From this it was clear that many managers have difficulty in placing their own operations in the national context. Some of the pieces of the planning jigsaw they know all too well from their own activities, but how these all fit together, and what the aims and objects of economic policy are, or should be, is not clear to them. Looking at the events of the 1960s in the economic policy field the one thing that emerges at all clearly is that the degree of government intervention in the running of the economy has increased and will continue to do so. This means that business decision-making is more and more affected by economic policy. The 'gentlemen in Whitehall' may or may not know best, but what they say is increasingly important. The main change in the direction of the economy now compared with the post-war years is in the attempt to bring management and trade unions into the decision-making process.

As a Special Adviser seconded to the N.E.D. Office for a period I had an opportunity of seeing the new approach to managing the economy in operation under both Conservative and Labour Governments. The differences in concept and practice were very marked. The Conservatives set up N.E.D.C. as a means of devising alternatives to stop-go within the general framework of an economic policy in which the price mechanism played a dominant part. The Labour Government regarded economic planning as a central part of 'positive government' and saw the N.E.D.C. as an adjunct of the newly created Department of Economic Affairs, which could be useful in bringing management and trade unions into partnership with Government in the formulation and implementation of the National Plan. When this was dropped in July 1966, the Government moved over to a policy involving more and continuous intervention in the running of the economy. This was concerned with the removal of obstacles to economic growth and, although the methods used are a long way from anything in the proposals put forward by Selwyn Lloyd when the N.E.D.C. was started, the intention is again the same.

The background against which Government economic policies have been formed and carried out in the 1960s has been one of great complexity. Confusion about Government intentions and competence has been increased by the impact of external events on domestic policy. Failure to enter the E.E.C. in 1963, the Korean War and its repercussions on the dollar and the international monetary system, Rhodesian sanctions and the Suez War with their impact on overseas trade, these are some of the events which have made this a period of sustained near-crisis. At home they have been marked by the introduction of various 'packages' of deflationary measures, notably those of 20th July 1966, and the record-making budget of March 1968. Following as it did the devaluation of the pound, and the gold crisis culminating in the I.M.F. emergency measures of March 1968, Mr. Jenkins' Budget emphasised the fact that the British Government now has little room for manœuvre in planning its economic strategy.

Today the role of Government in the running of the economy is more direct than ever before in peacetime. For businessmen this means coping with a succession of policy objectives expressed in the form of directives, tax and other incentives, penalties, and exhortations to sell or buy, to train, to be adventurous, or to stand fast. All this requires a tremendous amount of activity by civil servants and special bodies of all kinds. Neither businessmen nor the electorate in general believe nowadays that inflation, high unemployment, continuing balance of payments deficits and other signs of economic ill-health are just bad luck. At elections the voters are invited to expect, if not miracles, at least a level of performance only just this side of perfection. Governments should not be surprised that they are expected to come up with the answers to our economic problems. It is at this level that broad economic concepts dealing with, for example, the level of consumer spending, come under the cross-fire from special interests.

The Prime Minister has to assess the balance of forces in the country, in his own party, and in the Cabinet in deciding on major economic policy changes. Some decisions, for example, the devaluation of the pound in November 1967, or squeezing some £923 million in extra taxation in Mr. Jenkins' Budget, are turning points in the management of the economy. These are changes in direction; the points at which it is accepted that actions and not promises alter economic life. Managing the British economy is a complicated task at the best of times. In the 1960s it has become, in spite of all the endeavours to bring management, trade unions and government into the process, an increasingly hazardous undertaking.

This book attempts to explain the machinery for carrying out economic policy, and the way it has developed in the 1960's.

I
The Management of the Economy

The planning versus private enterprise argument which had gone on during the time of the post-war Labour Governments ended with the General Election of 1951. Within the next decade it was assumed without too much discussion that planning was either undesirable, unnecessary or unworkable. In the early 1950s it certainly appeared that the kind of planning carried out by the Labour Government which had been based on the Economic Surveys, the Long-Term Programme and the work of the Economic Planning Board, had been overtaken by events. Conservative Chancellors, following Mr. R. A. Butler, tended to rely on monetary policy as a means of regulating the economy. If planning was mentioned it was only necessary to remark that 'the gentlemen in Whitehall did not know best' to secure a change of subject. With continued full employment and the ending of the acute shortages of the post-war period the emphasis in the management of the economy had shifted and the problem of organising production to that of willing what was produced. The apparatus of control which had been built up during the war years was dismantled and devices such as bulk purchase by Government departments of imported raw materials fell into disuse. There was considerable talk of the value of the private enterprise system and the need to remove any checks on its free operation.

As different Chancellors of the Exchequer succeeded each other in the Conservative Governments of the 1950s it became clear, however, that informed management of the economy was becoming increasingly necessary if a situation was to be avoided in which the balance of payments dominated economic policy. Economic forecasting went on in the Central Statistical Office and the Economic Section of the Treasury. This work, which started off as a largely technical exercise, involved other departments which were called upon to provide information as a basis for forecasts. A 'Working Party' which was set up to meet this need became in time an inter-Departmental Committee. The work of the Plowden Committee[1] set up to consider the machinery of Government resulted in a considerable overhaul of existing arrangements for carrying out economic policies. On the longer-term policy side it recommended that public expenditure should be forecast and considered comprehensively for five years at a time. The first of these forecasts was not in fact published until 1963 and covered the years for 1967–8.

The move away from economic planning was accompanied by increased reliance on monetary policy and a tendency to regard changes in Bank Rate as a policy in themselves rather than a means to an end. The attempt to control output and prices by successively inflating and deflating demand by so-called stop-go policies made it extremely difficult for economic growth to take place. Difficulties over the balance of payments led to increasing reliance on internal deflation as a principal regulator of the economy whenever pressure on resources showed signs of getting out of hand. The result of this starting and stopping was that the economy never reached a point where sustained growth was possible. Another difficulty was the lack of information about the effects of particular changes of policy on the behaviour of the economy. No one knew what the impact of specific changes in direct and indirect taxation would be or the reaction of different sectors of the economy to measures taken and the length of time required for their operation.

A combination of full employment at home with recurrent balance of payments crises led to considerable confusion over the true position—the strengths and weaknesses—of the British economy. At various times different scapegoats were named for

[1] See p. 51.

the general lack of progress. Among these were the restrictive practices of the trade unions, unenterprising management, the maintenance of an over-valued pound, an unduly high level of social security benefits, excessive Government spending on defence, over-generous aid and technical assistance programmes for developing countries, over-full employment and a variety of technical defects in British industry, particularly in its export activities. At the same time the Federation of British Industry[1] and other bodies pointed out at intervals that British exports were highly competitive and that a greater proportion of the national income were exported by Britain than by any other country. However, Britain's share of world trade fell steadily throughout the 1950s while, particularly in the latter part of the period, imports of manufactured goods rose steadily.

The general desire to make a new approach to the problem of solving Britain's economic difficulties led to the search for new ways of managing the economy and this is the subject of this book. The activity falls into four broad phases. The first was characterised by the setting up of the National Economic Development Council by the Macmillan Government, to carry out what might be called indicative planning. The second phase, following the change of Government in October 1964, was marked by the setting up of the Department of Economic Affairs and the Ministry of Technology and the preparation and publication of the National Plan. The third phase began in July 1966 when the National Plan had to be abandoned because of the continuing balance of payments crisis. This phase was dominated by the need to build up exports in order to bring the balance of payments into surplus and if possible the repayment of the large sums borrowed from the International Monetary Fund and other organisations. The principal focus of attention at this time was on measures to change the structure of the economy. The fourth phase began in August 1967 when the Prime Minister took over responsibility for economic policy. This decision was followed in November by the announcement that the Government had decided to devalue the pound. It was hoped that devaluation would give a consid-

[1] It did not become the Confederation of British Industry until 1965.

erable boost to exports and that the fact that imports would be dearer would automatically cut down their consumption. A further loan was obtained from the International Monetary Fund on the understanding that deflationary measures would be taken sufficient to bring the economy under control. Two weeks after the devaluation decision Mr. Callaghan resigned as Chancellor of the Exchequer to be succeeded by Mr. Roy Jenkins.

As Chancellor throughout the first three years of the Wilson Government, Mr. Callaghan had carried out what proved to be an unsuccessful fight for the pound. Considerable discussion has taken place as to whether the pound should have been devalued at an earlier stage in the life of the Labour Government. The first occasion was clearly after the October Election when it would have been politically feasible to blame the devaluation on the inherited balance of payments deficit which in the moment of victory could have been described as the legacy of 'the thirteen wasted years'. Against this was the fact that the Government had a very small majority and the argument that it would be bad for the Labour Party to be labelled as the Devaluation Party in view of its action in 1931 and again in 1949. Devaluation was again a strong possibility in July 1966 when a number of events, including the Seamen's Strike, led to a run on the pound. As it was, the Prime Minister decided to introduce stringent deflationary measures which in the event failed to restore confidence abroad or to bring the balance of payments into surplus.

This decision brought in a period during which the Government was driven to first one and then another deflationary measure to protect the balance of payments with consequent increases in the level of unemployment. When reflation was attempted the effect on sterling was immediately disastrous.

The fact that the balance of payments dominated the economic scene in the years following the 1964 Election created an extremely confused situation. The setting up of the Department of Economic Affairs and the consequent division of control over economic policy between it and the Treasury introduced the new factor into the management of the economy. Following

4

the policy of Mr. Maudling, who had been Chancellor up to the General Election, the Government had attempted to introduce a period of faster economic growth using the reserves and foreign borrowing to tide over the period until productivity would have increased sufficiently to bring the payments situation into balance. This meant that the economy ran at a very high level of activity throughout 1965 and the first half of 1966. It was hoped that the various direct measures introduced to help the balance of payments would keep down the deficit and eliminate it altogether by the end of 1966. However, in the event this did not prove possible. Demand remained higher than had been expected in spite of the various deflationary measures taken on 20th July 1966 and earlier. Perhaps the principal reason for this was the very high level of public investment which was taking place. Another was the failure to hold back wages, combined with comparative success in holding back prices. The continuing high level of Government spending overseas was a further factor in a situation in which it was all too easy for the economy to be 'blown off course'.

All this meant that the growth programme started by the Conservative Government with the setting up of the National Economic Development Council had come to an end. Britain had received generous international financial support for the pound which clearly could not be continued without evidence that the Government was prepared to give top priority to putting right the balance of payments whatever the cost might be to the rate of growth. The Government had been committed to trying to hold down home demand by keeping unemployment above a level of 2 per cent. All the measures which the Government had decided to introduce were long-term in their effects. They included the revision of the defence policy, the withdrawal of troops from 'East of Suez' commitments, the various measures for changing the structure of the economy, the possibility of reducing the cost of the social services by the introduction of means tests—the so-called move towards selectivity—all needed time to take effect. By 18th November 1967 the Government had no room for manœuvre and devaluation was inevitable.

ECONOMIC POLICY MACHINERY

From the time of the publication of the Employment Policy White Paper of 1944, the economic thinking of successive governments was dominated by the Keynesian emphasis on regulating demand. The result was that in no year since 1947 did unemployment in the United Kingdom reach as much as 3 per cent. In the same period prices doubled, but although this was undoubtedly a considerable rise, it was not raging inflation. In the 1950s inadequate growth rates were blamed on stop-go management of the economy. The balance of payments was given as the main constraint on growth and the periodic sterling crises were responsible for the restraints of the stop period. The shift of emphasis to the need for faster economic growth was to result in an entirely new concept of management for the economy. Not so long ago the position was relatively simple. The Treasury, subject only to pressure exerted by the Cabinet or Prime Minister, had sole official responsibility for economic policy. The Bank of England looked after sterling and the supply of money, the Board of Trade took care of industry and commerce and dealt with tariffs and trade and various other matters. The Ministry of Labour attended to wages and hours of work, strikes, lock-outs and conditions of employment. Farther out on the fringes of economic policy, particular Ministries dealt with transport, aircraft production, housing and so on. The position has since become very much more complicated. Governments having increased their interest in economic affairs and expanded the volume of economic statute law have had to adjust the machinery accordingly. Endeavours to improve efficiency of industry depend on securing closer co-ordination of the activities of the public and private sectors. This was one of the objectives set out for the National Economic Development Council when it was established. The National Board for Prices and Incomes, the Monopolies Commission, the Restrictive Practices Court and the Industrial Reorganisation Corporation have all come into being as a result of the culmination of general Government policy allied to specific legislative measures. The creation of each of these new bodies can be understood easily enough in the light of the circumstances surrounding their creation. The Industrial Reorganisation Corporation, for example, was created to enforce changes in the structure of industry arising from the work of various committees set up to investigate the shortcomings of particular sectors. These included the Geddes Committee on Shipbuilding, the Plowden Committee on the Aircraft Industry, the Rochdale Committee on Ports, as well as the reports of numerous 'Little Neddies' on specific problems. Other directions in which Government has intervened in the operation of the economy include measures to strengthen the computer industry, new arrangements for Government research and development contracts, directives on Government purchasing and their impact on industrial efficiency, changes in the law on Resale Price Maintenance, the whole apparatus of industrial training, business schools and regional economic planning.

The work of co-ordinating these varied activities has fallen on the Department of Economic Affairs and the Ministry of Technology. After the 1964 Election the Secretary of State for Economic Affairs had the task of co-ordinating the activities of Ministries through his position as chairman of the various key Ministerial committees which between them cover the broad range of economic and industrial policy. At the same time he had the task of ensuring that the various agencies which had been created operated effectively and enjoyed the support of the T.U.C., the C.B.I., and other bodies. From August 1967, when the Prime Minister took over responsibility for economic policy, until April 1968 when he relinquished it, the Department of Economic Affairs worked closely with the Cabinet Office. As chairman of the National Economic Development Council the Prime Minister took charge of various activities concerned with the removal of specific obstacles to growth.

With so many new organisations operating in the economic field and with existing ones taking on new functions it is extremely difficult for businessmen and others to keep track of what is going on. The confusion is increased by the fact that different agencies with overlapping functions can all be investigating the same topic. Industrial pricing policies, for example, can be discussed by the Restrictive Practices Court, the Monopolies Commission or the Prices and Incomes Board. To some extent this proliferation of organisations is inevitable. It is important that those called upon to serve on these bodies should be employing their time usefully and not duplicating the activities of others. Again it is not clear that the best use has always been made of the new agencies and especially the staffs which they have recruited. This is particularly so with organisations which can only deal with questions which are specifically referred to them. The Prices and Incomes Board, for example, can only act on references made to it. These generally concern a particular industry whereas there is no doubt that the Board is in a very good position to take a broader view involving the relationship between a number of industries.

This book will explain how the present system for managing the economy has been built up in Britain from the time of the setting up of the National Economic Development Council by the Conservative Government in 1962. In the years since then *ad hoc* planning has created a situation in which there has been a great deal of activity without co-ordinated action. Businessmen seeking the road through the planning labyrinth are at a loss to know which organisations are to be taken seriously and which are simply going through the motions. The events since the 1964 election have shown that the creation of new organisations does not necessarily mean the introduction of new policies. Nothing could have been more orthodox than the long defence of sterling by deflationary policies followed by the Labour Government, nothing more radical than the Conservative removal of Resale Price Maintenance.

II
The Machinery of Planning—
N.E.D.C. to D.E.A.

The introduction of planning to Britain can be conveniently dated from the first meeting of the National Economic Development Council in March 1962. It was part of a series of measures introduced by Mr. Selwyn Lloyd, then Chancellor of the Exchequer, for dealing with the balance of payments crisis. It represented the acceptance by the Government of the need for a faster rate of growth in the British economy, and its intention to involve both management and the trade unions in securing it. Dissatisfaction with the previous rate of growth, and even more with its uncertain and intermittent progress, in which stop inevitably followed go, was the driving force behind the new approach.

In deciding to set up a new organisation to take responsibility for drafting long-term plans the Chancellor was considerably influenced by the need for improving the basis of consultation and forecasting. At that time many Conservatives were sceptical of the wisdom of embarking on long-term planning and even those who were prepared to accept the need for a new approach felt that this must be in a form different from the Labour Party's planning operations of the 1940s. Among the free economy men it was possible to find a number who were against planning but believed that it was necessary to bring in people with knowledge and experience of industry to reinforce the efforts of the Treasury civil servants. Wartime precedents were held to justify this departure from normal constitutional practice which had already been tried out in the 'three Wise Men' approach of the Committee on Prices and

Incomes. Selwyn Lloyd himself declared as a justification for setting up the N.E.D.C. that he would like to have a source of advice available other than what came to him from the Treasury, so that he would be in a better position to weigh up the priorities of the situation.

In view of all that has happened since it is interesting to see what Selwyn Lloyd had in mind when he announced to the House of Commons his intention of setting up a new body.

On 26th July 1961, speaking in the Commons, he plunged boldly into the planning controversy and showed a grasp of the problem that justifies quotation of his speech at some length:

I will deal first with growth in the economy. The controversial matter of planning at once arises. I am not frightened of the word. One of the first things I did when appointed Chancellor was to ask for a plan of the programme for development and expenditure in the public sector for five years ahead. I referred to the problem as affecting the economy as a whole, in my speech in the economic debate last February. I have thought about it a great deal since and discussed it with representatives of both sides of industry. In addition to plans in the public sector, including those of the various nationalised industries and plans for certain industries in the private sector, developments in the economy as a whole are studied by a number of bodies. These include the Economic Planning Board presided over by the Permanent Secretary to the Treasury, the National Production Advisory Council on Industry over which I preside, and various other advisory councils.

I think the time has come for a better co-ordination of these various activities. I intend to discuss urgently with both sides of industry procedures for pulling together these various processes of consultation and forecasting with a view to better co-ordination of ideas and plans. I stated some time ago that I thought that an annual increase of 3 per cent in the gross national product was feasible, but only if we have a 6 per cent annual expansion of exports. I want to discuss with both sides of industry the implications of this kind of target for the various sectors of the economy.[1]

The emphasis on the need to expand exports in order to

[1] *Hansard*, 26th July 1961, Cols. 220–1.

secure faster growth was an important feature of the Chancellor's proposal. As will be seen later the N.E.D.C. Report *Growth of the United Kingdom Economy to 1966* (published in February 1963) decided that a 5 per cent increase over the years from 1961 to 1966 was required. This was increased to 5·1 per cent in September when the growth estimates were re-examined by the N.E.D.C. in *The Growth of the Economy* (published in March 1964).

In the discussion of the type of organisation that the N.E.D.C. was to be, the Chancellor made it clear that it would go beyond the function of the advisory bodies already in existence.

In the speech already quoted he went on to say:

I envisage a joint examination of the economic prospects of the country stretching five or more years into the future. It would cover the growth of national production and distribution of our resources between the main uses, consumption, Government expenditure, investment, and so on. Above all, it would try to establish what are the essential conditions for realising potential growth.

That covers, first, the supply of labour and capital, secondly, the balance of payments conditions and the development of imports and exports, and, thirdly, the growth of incomes. In other words, I want both sides of industry to share with the Government the task of relating plans to the resources likely to be available.[1]

The actual setting up of the National Economic Development Council did not take place until March of the following year. In the meantime, a series of meetings took place between the Chancellor and the employers' organisations—the Federation of British Industry, the British Employers' Confederation, the National Union of British Manufacturers—and with the T.U.C. On the 23rd September 1961 the Chancellor published the text of a letter which he had sent to the T.U.C. and the various management organisations. This read as follows:

Following upon my meetings with both sides of industry about a new approach to economic planning on a national scale, I have given careful thought to the various suggestions which have been

[1] *Hansard*, Col. 439—26th July 1961.

made. In order to forward our joint consideration of these matters, I set out in this letter, as promised, some specific proposals.

I believe that the time has come to establish new and more effective machinery for the co-ordination of plans and forecasts for the main sectors of our economy. There is a need to study centrally the plans and prospects of our main industries, to correlate them with each other and with the Government's plans for the public sector, and to see how in aggregate they contribute to, and fit in with, the prospects for the economy as a whole, including the vital external balance of payments. The task of keeping claims on our resources within our capacity is the responsibility of Government. But experience has shown the need for a closer link between Government and industry in order to create a climate favourable to expansion and to make possible effective action to correct weaknesses in our economic structure. This new machinery should therefore assist in the promotion of more rapid and sustained economic growth.

I am anxious to secure that both sides of industry, on whose co-operation the fulfilment of our objectives must significantly depend, should participate fully with the Government in all stages of the process. I hope they would, under the arrangements proposed below, obtain a picture, more continuous and comprehensive than has hitherto been available, of the long-term problems in the development of our economy; and this should enhance the value of their advice on, and efforts in, the search for solutions. They would also have better opportunities to help in the moulding of the economic policies of the Government at the formative stage.

Clearly, we shall need some new machinery for this work. I envisage that this might take the following form. First, I propose the creation of a National Economic Development Council. The Chancellor of the Exchequer would be the Chairman and one or two other Ministers, such as the President of the Board of Trade and the Minister of Labour, would be members. The other members of the Council, who would be appointed by the Chancellor after appropriate consultations, would be drawn from the trade unions and from the management side of private and nationalised industry, with perhaps some additional members. I would aim at a total membership of, say, about twenty.

The functions of the Council would be to examine and, if necessary, commission studies relevant to the economic objectives which I have indicated earlier in this letter, and to consider how these objectives could best be secured. Responsibility for final decisions on matters of Government policy must remain with the Government, but the view expressed by the Council would carry great weight both with the Government and with industry. It would be for the Council to consider how far, and in what form, the results of its work should be made public.

The effectiveness of the Council's work would depend on the establishment of a full-time staff of the right calibre. This staff, which would work under a director to be appointed from outside the civil service, although under the aegis of Government, would not be part of the ordinary Government machine. It would act under the general direction of, and be responsible to, the Council. The Government for their part would be prepared to make available from the civil service an appropriate portion of the staff. I would hope that the rest would be drawn from both sides of industry, the commercial world and elsewhere. Normally individual members of the staff would be regarded as on temporary secondment for, say, two or three years.

The function of this staff would be to examine the plans for development of the main industries in the private sector and, in the light of such examinations and of discussions with Government Departments about other sectors of the economy, e.g. the nationalised industries, to prepare, for the consideration of the Council, studies of the kind envisaged in the second paragraph of this letter. The staff would make the fullest use of existing channels of information and consultation in Government and industry, and in the studies of particular industries would work in association with the Government departments and other public bodies, e.g. the Iron and Steel Board and the Cotton Board, normally concerned with them.

The Chancellor did not, however, wait until the agreement of both sides of industry had been secured before going on to put his idea into practice. In a debate on Incomes and Productivity in the House of Commons on the 18th December he announced the appointment of Sir Robert Shone as Director General of the National Economic Development Office. Sir Robert, a distinguished economist who at that time was Executive Member of the Iron and Steel Board, was a man with considerable practical experience in industry as well as a first-hand acquaintance with the working of the Government machine. At this time the bringing in of prominent figures from industry for full-time appointments in Government service was something that had rarely happened since the end of the Second World War. This appointment was therefore of considerable importance to the success of the attempt to line up both sides of industry in consultation with Government. There were those who saw the setting up of the National Econonomic Development Office as the coming into existence of a new centre of economic power which would be a rival to the Treasury. This in fact did not happen for reasons which have been described very fully elsewhere.[1]

However, the N.E.D.C. concept served as a focus for the various ideas which together formed the great reappraisal of economic policy which took place in the years after the 1959 General Election. The famous conference on 'The next five years', organised by the Federation of British Industries (in November 1960), was regarded as the first indication that British businessmen were beginning to take an interest in problems of faster economic growth and ways and means by which this could be brought about. The impetus to this movement was given by Mr. (now Sir) Hugh Weeks, the Chairman of the F.B.I. Economic Policy Committee who was Chairman of the Industrial and Commercial Finance Corporation, a body set up by various banks and other City organisations for financing small firms. In particular the report of Group III at the F.B.I. Conference dealing with economic growth in Britain had put forward the view, in contradiction of the Government policy expounded at the conference by Viscount Amory, a former Chancellor of the Exchequer, that the achievement of a faster rate of economic growth might be the means of securing stable prices and a sound balance of payments. Viscount Amory had put the priorities the other way round.

This view was not official F.B.I. policy at that time but it is important as an indication of the way in which an intellectual minority among British businessmen was beginning to make its voice heard. At the same time discussion had been going on in the Treasury about the ways in which economic policy was

[1] See *The Treasury under the Tories, 1951–1964*, by Samuel Brittan, Penguin Books.

formulated and the possibility of improving these. Studies were made of French planning methods and various officials paid unobtrusive visits to Paris to study its organisation at first hand. The idea of setting up an independent planning organisation outside the Treasury was not greeted with enthusiasm by other members of the Cabinet, and was certainly unpopular in the Treasury itself. However, it was clear to Selwyn Lloyd that if industry was to take any notice of the activities of the planning body it must itself be involved through its official representatives. This explains why the unusual step was taken of creating an organisation outside the orbit of the Treasury establishment, headed by a Director General from outside the civil service, and intended to examine economic policy with criteria based on a different order of priorities and a different set of objectives. At the time the setting up of the N.E.D.C. had all the appearance of a victory for a new radical approach to economic policy-making, involving the fundamental conception of partnership between Government, management and trade unions.

The T.U.C. hesitated for several months before agreeing on 24th February 1962 to participate in the work of the N.E.D.C. The difficulties which it experienced in coming to a decision were concerned both with procedures and policies. On the procedural side the T.U.C. insisted that trade union members of the Council should be regarded as sitting as representatives of their organisations and that they should be free to report back to them on the work of the Council. The T.U.C. was very strongly against having large numbers of independents on the Council and insisted that it should be a small tightly knit body representing major interest groups in the country. On the policy side the T.U.C., while agreeing that the best hope for solving the problems of the British economy lay in securing faster economic growth, hesitated to ally itself with the view that wage restraint would be any solution to our economic difficulties.

The main points in the argument between the Chancellor and the T.U.C. are contained in the extracts from the correspondence between them given below.

On 10th January 1962 Mr. Selwyn Lloyd wrote to the T.U.C. setting out the objectives of his economic policy, and in the course of his letter referred to the N.E.D.C. as follows:

I cannot let pass the opportunity of emphasising to you once again my belief in the importance of the work of this N.E.D. Council and the great opportunity which it provides for the two sides of industry to influence policy, to tackle in co-operation with the Government the obstacles to sound growth, and to consider with us the availability and use or misuse of resources. I ask you once again, as a body which has consistently urged upon me the advantages of such co-ordination of economic effort, to join in this work.

When the Council is established I will place before it papers on the prospects of the United Kingdom economy for the next five years and on the problems of economic growth and national efficiency, and will suggest that as one of its early actions the Council should instruct its staff, in collaboration with the main industries, to examine the long-term prospects of these industries, their requirements for investment and skilled manpower and their expectations as to production and exports. The results would then be correlated with each other and with the Government's plans for the public sector, to provide a basis for future action.

On the 24th February the T.U.C. replied to this letter, setting out views critical of the Government's economic policy but expressing a readiness to serve on the Council.

The General Council are very conscious of the difficulties of Britain's economic position, and are as anxious as the Government to find a solution for those difficulties. They are, however, convinced that neither the interests of the nation nor, more particularly, those of working people would be best served by the alternative policies put forward by the Chancellor. The only correct approach lies in the adoption of positive measures to secure sustained expansion. The possibility that this might be achieved by participating in the National Economic Development Council has been carefully examined by the General Council in considering the invitation to be represented on that body.

The General Council are still by no means free of the doubts which they have already expressed to the Chancellor about the probable effectiveness of the proposed machinery. Nevertheless, having taken note of the Chancellor's assurances that the N.E.D.C. would be consulted before the Government formed its policy on economic issues and that it would be competent to initiate discussions and to make recommendations on any subject, and anxious not to impede any opportunity of securing a collective effort to achieve more rapid progress in a context of full employment and rising living standards, they are prepared to accept the invitation. In doing so, they wish to emphasise that they attach great importance to the right of the members of the Council to report to the organisations which they represent, and that they would not regard associations with the Council as debarring those organisations from expressing in public such reservations as they might hold about government decisions on economic policy. Moreover, as the General Council have made clear in the preceding paragraphs, this decision does not imply acceptance of the Chancellor's view that the solution to Britain's economic difficulties is to be found in wage restraint.

As a result of Mr. Selwyn Lloyd's endeavours the National Economic Development Council was eventually formed and its membership announced on the 8th February 1962. The initial membership of twenty consisted of two independents and three groups representing management, the trade unions, and the Government.

The names of the original members of the Council are given in Appendix II.

There were no permanent officials of the Treasury as members of the Council and the only official allowed to take part in the proceedings was the Director General of the N.E.D. Office who was included in the membership.

The N.E.D. Office was established in the old St. Stephen's Club on the Thames Embankment just opposite Big Ben. In former days Conservative M.P.s were able to hurry back from the club for Divisions along an underground passage. The Office enjoyed no such speedy access to Parliament and its affairs. Again, although the salaries of its members were paid from public funds and their activities bound by the provisions of the Official Secrets Act, they remained very much on the outside of Government activity. The concept of the N.E.D.C. as an independent organisation meant that its officials had no right of access to official documents or to discussions taking place on economic policy within the Treasury. In fact as time went on it became clear that the members of the N.E.D. Office were having the worst of both worlds. Those who joined its staff from industry, the universities and elsewhere, were usually engaged on a two-year contract whose terms were limited by civil service ideas of what was appropriate to their stations. The combination of low salaries, short-term contracts and no pension arrangements combined to place a premium on dedication as a qualification for service in the N.E.D. Office.

From the start the Office was organised into two broad divisions, Economic and Industrial. The Economic Division was concerned with general and particular issues of economic policy and was responsible for making the calculations and projections on which the N.E.D.C. growth programme was based. The Industrial Division was concerned with the performance and problems of separate industries or industrial sectors. Its members were for the most part recruited from industry and their ability to carry on what was called a 'running dialectic' between the economic and industrial worlds was regarded as important. Indeed it was as a means of bridging the gulf between the civil service and industry that the N.E.D. Office was believed to have its greatest value. In the period up to October 1964 the Office also included special sections dealing respectively with science and technology, and with manpower and training.

Looking back, it is difficult to realise the enthusiasm which this strange organisation, working amidst the fading splendours of the old St. Stephen's Club, generated amongst business economists, the press, and in the universities. It represented the best hope of the long-awaited reappraisal of economic policy and as such was acceptable to both Right and Left shades of political thinking. The Right saw here the possibility of a rejuvenation of the market mechanism through the application of commonsense ideas acceptable to management, trade unions and Government. This was to be planning without a vast superstructure of Government interference in the running of industry. To the Left the setting up of the N.E.D.C. was seen as a recognition of the limitations of the free-market system and the ending of the belief which had been fashionable in Conservative circles in the early 1950s that the economy could be run with just two regulators, the foreign exchange rate and the Bank Rate. To the general public the N.E.D.C. appeared as an organisation embodying the classic principle of British politics that all problems can be solved if only the interested parties can be brought together round a table to discuss them. Few new departures in British political life have set off with so much general goodwill surrounding their activities. Few, as events were to show, can have been launched less well equipped to deal with the tasks allotted to them.

HOW THE N.E.D.C. WORKED

The first meeting of the National Economic Development Council took place on the 7th March 1962. The Chancellor of the Exchequer, who acted as Chairman of the Council, explained in general terms what was expected of it. These, according to a statement issued after the meeting, were as follows:

(a) To examine the economic performance of the nation with particular concern for plans for the future in both the private and public sectors of industry.

(b) To consider together what are the obstacles to quicker growth, what can be done to improve efficiency, and whether the best use is being made of our resources.

(c) To seek agreement upon ways of improving economic performance, competitive power and efficiency, in other words, to increase the rate of sound growth.

I have tried to make it clear from the beginning that I would not seek to exclude any subject from our discussions, and that I would not arrogate to Ministers the right to fix the agenda. I do not want this to be a body which just listens to Government decisions, and is merely asked for comment. I want it to have an important impact on Government policy during the formative stage, and upon the economic life of the nation. I believe that it can.

These objectives seemed to be sensible and logical. What the Council was being asked to do was to find out by collecting information, making projections, consulting with industry and the trade unions and in other ways, exactly how the economy was performing. Having done this it was in its collective wisdom to decide how the economy could be made to work more efficiently, and whether the best use was being made of the resources available. From this recommendations for action would follow. The Council's task was therefore both fact-finding and policy-making. Difficulties arose, however, on both aspects of this dual approach.

In considering the work that the Office did at this time it must be remembered that it was beginning virtually from scratch. The process of starting up a department of this kind is extremely complicated. At one end the administrative machinery was set up on civil service lines and rules laid down about the size of the establishment, the rank of the various officials, scales of salaries, length of engagement, followed by the humdrum arrangements about office accommodation, furniture, and so on. The man responsible for this part of the operation of setting up the N.E.D.C. was Mr. Frank Pickford, an Under-Secretary seconded from the Ministry of Labour.

The other end of the operation consisted in the recruitment of economists, and others, to work on the preparation of the plan, collect information from industry and advise the Council on technical matters. The recruitment of these people had to be done from the top downwards, and little progress could be made until the appointments of the Economic Director and Industrial Director. Both of these had been made by the time of the first meeting of the Council. Sir Donald MacDougall, who was appointed Economic Director, had worked in the Economic Secretariat during the war and been the chief adviser in the Prime Minister's Statistical Branch from 1951 to 1953. After leaving the Government service he had pursued a distinguished academic career and was the author of a well-known book *The World Dollar Problem* and an authority on Commonwealth Preference. Mr. T. C. Fraser, who was appointed Industrial Director, came from the trade association world, having been Secretary General of the Wool Textile Delegation at Bradford. The members of the staff were recruited partly from industry, the universities, the trade unions, trade associations, research bodies and so on. Those seconded from the civil service were for the most part volunteers who had agreed to accept service in this hybrid organisation. The business of fitting people with such varied backgrounds and temperaments together was far from easy. The position was made more difficult in many ways when the Office moved to the Millbank Tower in the summer of 1963. The difficulty was one of vertical geography. The Economic Section was on one floor, the Industrial Section on another and the Director General and the administrative secretary, press, publicity and various advisers all on yet another. The result of this stratification was to make communication more difficult between different sections of the office than it might otherwise have been. This sort of thing happens in Government departments and big organisations of all kinds but it was unfortunate that the N.E.D. Office, which was kept down to a staff of around one hundred, should have had communication problems added on to its other difficulties.

The position of the N.E.D.C. on the edge of the administrative machinery was in any case a difficult one. Contact with management and the trade unions came relatively easily through the staff members who had come in from industry. Contact with Government departments was more difficult. There was no great enthusiasm in some of the sponsoring departments for attempts by the N.E.D. Office to establish working relations with what they regarded as 'their' industries. This difficulty was particularly marked when the Economic Development Committees came to be set up in the following year. Endless man-hours were spent writing papers for some Ministries to explain exactly what the Industrial Department was doing. These delays were especially frustrating to men who had held important positions in industry and elsewhere and had joined the Office under the impression that they were to form a task force for improving Britain's economic performance.

C

Selwyn Lloyd's idea of setting up an independent body which was under the aegis of, but not in, the Government was by any standards a difficult one to carry out. In practice the major shortcomings proved to be on the side of the Government machinery.

The composition of the Council also gave rise to difficulties. The T.U.C. had insisted that its members serving on the Council should be representatives of the trade union movement and able to report back to their members on what the Council was doing. For them the independent status of the N.E.D.C. was regarded as a condition of their participation. One of the main reasons why Mr. Selwyn Lloyd insisted that the N.E.D. Office must be distinct from the Treasury was that such a body, enjoying a wide measure of independence, would be more likely to secure the confidence of the trade unions.

On the management side the problem was in many ways more difficult. At that time there was not a single organisation representing management in the way that the T.U.C. spoke for the trade unions. Questions of wages and hours of work were the concern of the British Employers' Confederation while problems of trade and industrial organisation were dealt with, so far as the large companies were concerned, by the Federation of British Industries and the small firms by the National Union of British Manufacturers. This division by size and function made representation at the national level difficult. The management side of the Council at its first inception consisted of what might be called 'representative managers' rather than representatives of management. The contrast between their position and that of the T.U.C. members was to be seen in the preliminaries before Council meetings took place. On the first Wednesday of the month, when the Council met, the T.U.C. members were shown into a private room on arrival where presumably they discussed together the business of the meeting. The management members went straight into the Council room and chatted about the weather, the Budget or whatever else was engaging their attention at the time. It was only after the formation of the Confederation of British Industry in 1965 that the management side, having become representative of a wide spectrum of industrial companies and interests, held pre-Council meetings of its own.

The effect of this constitutional difference on the role of the Council can easily be imagined. The T.U.C. members were able to put up a united view on problems in which they were particularly interested, such as the attempt by Mr. Maudling in the spring of 1964 to secure agreement on a voluntary prices and incomes policy. At the same time they made very valuable contributions to the discussion of papers prepared by the Office on specific problems. The management members were left with the alternatives of putting forward F.B.I. views, attempting to put across ideas and solutions of their own, or looking for ways and means of changing the organisation and making it more effective. In this last category the moving spirit was Mr. Reay Geddes, Managing Director of Dunlop, who had taken a leading part in the discussions at the F.B.I. Brighton Conference. Unfortunately, the various initiatives which he proposed came to nothing and he left the Council in 1964 to become Chairman of the Inquiry into the Shipbuilding Industry.

1964 AND THE DEPARTMENT OF ECONOMIC AFFAIRS

In June 1963, Mr. Harold Wilson, speaking at the annual conference of the Transport and General Workers' Union, had stated that the Labour Party believed in 'Neddy' but 'a Neddy made into a reality with the Socialist policies which alone can turn an academic exercise into a National Plan'. When the Labour Government took office in mid-October 1964 it was to be expected, therefore, that changes would take place in the arrangements for carrying out economic growth policy. Throughout the summer of 1964 the N.E.D. Office had continued to work on the preliminary estimates for the follow-up to the growth programme which was to cover the years 1967 to 1970. No publications of any importance appeared and there was a general atmosphere of *festine lente* about its operations. Although Mr. Wilson had expressed his belief in Neddy, plans for reorganising the economic Ministries had been widely discussed and it was known that Neddy would never be the same again. The Election affected it both in the organi-

sation of the Office and its relations with Government departments, and in the composition of the Council itself. The changes
in the Office took place almost immediately on the results of
the General Election being known. The Department of
Economic Affairs was set up on the 16th October, two days after
the Election and, in the words of the first issue of its monthly
bulletin *Progress Report*, it 'began work the same evening'. The
N.E.D. Office staff read in their newspapers of changes
affecting its senior members, but the full extent of what was
happening did not become clear until the Office opened on the
morning of Monday, the 18th October. Those arriving a little
late that morning met former colleagues hurrying away from
the building, their more portable possessions under their arms,
on their way to take posts in the new Department of Economic
Affairs. The main cause of confusion was that no one quite
knew who had actually gone, who was going and who was going
to be left. This uncertainty continued for several days. The
position was complicated by the fact that the N.E.D. Office
staff had been recruited from industry, universities and elsewhere to work under a Conservative administration. Some of
them, therefore, inevitably regarded the changes that were
taking place with disfavour. Others, however, were elated at
the results of the Election and were now looking forward to the
introduction of measures to provide the organisation with
'teeth' which had been promised in the Election campaign.
There was, however, a feeling of being left out of things among
the staff remaining as first one and then another of their colleagues were sent for to report at Storeys Gate.

The principal changes made in the N.E.D. Office were the
result of taking the planning process inside the Government.
This meant that the greater part of the Economic Section,
with its Director General, Sir Donald MacDougall, moved
over to the new department, together with the Adviser on
Training and Labour questions. The Scientific Adviser moved
downstairs in the Millbank Tower to the newly formed Ministry
of Technology. The changes in the Council were made with
much less expedition. Mr. George Brown, the First Secretary
of State and Minister for Economic Affairs, was too preoc-

cupied with the very exacting task of forming an entirely new Ministry from scratch to give much thought to the composition of what was now a purely advisory body. The Council was not called together in November and did not meet again till early December, nearly two months after the Election. When it did meet a number of significant changes had taken place in the Ministerial membership. The Minister for Economic Affairs was now Chairman instead of the Chancellor of the Exchequer. The Minister of Labour and the President of the Board of Trade remained as members and to them was added the Minister of Technology in the person of Mr. Frank Cousins, who had previously sat as a T.U.C. representative. Another change was the appearance on the Council of the Industrial Adviser to the Government, Mr. Fred Catherwood, as an ex-officio member. The management, trade union and independent members took their places as before, with only minor changes in personnel.

Under the new arrangement there were clearly advantages for the Government in keeping the Industrial Division of the N.E.D. Office outside the new department in an independent position. The planning function following on the work of forecasting and investigation which had been carried out by the Economic Section of the N.E.D. Office would now be carried out within the Ministry. However, the Government was anxious to keep N.E.D.C. as a ready-made independent forum for discussion of economic matters, especially those affecting the trade unions and industry. Both management and the trade unions could see advantages in being able to talk to the Government through an independent Council rather than calling as *ad hoc* delegations at the Department of Economic Affairs. From the Minister's point of view there were advantages in being able to refer to a separate body which would reflect local pressures and interests. At the same time, the Economic Development Committees, the 'Little Neddies', took on a new importance as collectors of information necessary for the National Plan, and as instruments for securing its implementation.

The functions of the National Economic Development

Council under the new administration were explained by Mr. George Brown in a House of Commons debate. He stated:

Under the policy which we intend to pursue for more purposive economic planning, it is evident that the responsibility must lie with the Government themselves. Therefore this work will be carried out in future in my department, in close co-operation with the Treasury, and other Government departments concerned. There is nevertheless a continuing need for an outside body on which representatives of industry and commerce can discuss the Government's economic plans at the various stages of their formulation, can contribute to their formulation and can discuss more generally policies directed to securing economic growth, particularly those dependent on the understanding and co-operation of industry, and, finally, a body to provide a proper channel of communication with individual industries for the purpose of securing that the implications of the National Plan are understood in each industry and that the circumstances of each industry are understood in the preparation of the Plan.

It is for these purposes that we propose to reconstitute the National Economic Development Council on very much its former basis, with a membership composed of Government, management and trade unions, and a small number of individual members. The Council, as hitherto, will be served by its own staff in the N.E.D. Office and I have invited Sir Robert Shone to continue in the office of Director General.[1]

This statement put an end to rumours about the future of the National Economic Development Council and its Office.

[1] *Hansard*, House of Commons, 4 November 1964.

III
The N.E.D.C. Growth Programme

At the second meeting of the N.E.D. Council on the 9th May 1962 it was decided that the main task should be the preparation of a report studying the implications of an average annual growth rate of 4 per cent for the period 1961 to 1966, that is, of nearly 22 per cent over the whole period. It was agreed that the staff should carry out an inquiry with a selected cross-section of industry in the public and private sectors on the impact of a 4 per cent growth rate on them. The inquiry would also study the general economic implications of faster growth for the main components of the national economy, that is, manpower, investment and the balance of payments. The scope of the inquiry was limited by the information available and the short time which the Office could be allowed for gathering material. This was reflected in the selection of industries from those which, for the most part, were thought most likely to be able to provide the information required quickly and accurately.[1] The idea of a 4 per cent growth rate was accepted with apparent satisfaction by the public at large. There was little realisation of the difficulties to be overcome in the process of achieving such a rate and a tendency to suppose that simply by taking sufficient thought the Government, assisted, of course, by the N.E.D.C., would be able to add 4 per cent per annum to the nation's G.N.P.

[1] The industries selected were:
   Public: coal; gas; electricity; Post Office.
   Private: agriculture; chemicals; chocolate and sugar confectionery; building; civil engineering and building materials; heavy electrical machinery; electronics; iron and steel; machine tools; motor vehicles; paper and board; petroleum; wool textiles.

The actual figure of 4 per cent had not simply been taken from a hat but was based on the ten-year target of a 50 per cent growth rate agreed by the O.E.C.D. in 1962. This compared with an annual increase of 3 per cent which the economy was then assumed to be achieving according to Treasury estimates. Also 4 per cent was thought to be a sufficient challenge for industry and at the same time not too high to discourage effort while remaining realistic. During 1962 the 4 per cent growth rate was promoted in political speeches and in the press from being an estimate of what might be possible to becoming a target to be achieved. The proclamation of the 4 per cent growth rate was a considerable achievement for the N.E.D. Office. Anything less would have been tantamount to accepting the views which had prevailed in the Treasury over the past decade and admitting that improvement was not possible except in the very long term. The N.E.D. Office regarded 4 per cent as on the low side and was anxious to prove that it could be achieved and indeed surpassed. The Treasury view was that it was on the high side, but as it was a N.E.D.C. concept saw no harm to itself if the economy failed to attain it. The Government saw in a 4 per cent growth rate the prospect of an end to stop-go, and the electoral advantages which would follow from a period of expansion. In industry there was considerable optimism, as revealed by the industrial inquiry, regarding the possibility of achieving the 4 per cent objective. As Sir Robert Shone pointed out at a later stage it was the fact that industry accepted the 4 per cent objective that made it possible for the N.E.D.C. to go ahead and prepare the first plan, without running into unmanageable bottlenecks, either of manpower or of capital investment, and that it proved possible to issue the growth programme in the first year of the Council's existence.

However, there is much more to the preparation of a plan than deciding on an overall growth rate. It is necessary to put forward in concrete terms the changes which faster growth will bring about. These need to be expressed in terms of living standards, better education, additional housing, better transport facilities, and all the other things which the public at large expect to arrive with growth. There is, of course, a chicken-

and-egg relationship between faster growth and improved standards. Do we get faster growth because the education system has been improved or are we able to build better schools and spend more money on education because faster growth makes it possible? Where a specific practical problem is involved, for example the need for increased supplies of energy, these have to be dealt with before the faster growth can be achieved. But it must be remembered that their inputs and outputs have their human as well as their factory level with, in Sir Robert Shone's words, 'the whole process expanding and broadening as the scale of output rises and the standards and horizons of life develop and widen'.[1]

The N.E.D.C. Plan—*Growth of the United Kingdom Economy 1961–6*—was published in February 1963. This was not by any standards a time when hopes were running high either on the political or economic front. The economy was in recession, General de Gaulle had a month before vetoed the British application for membership of the Common Market, and the country was going through a period of exceptionally cold weather. To some extent therefore the N.E.D.C. growth programme was seen as the light at the end of the tunnel and as such was given a good send off. Apart from anything else, it brought together a great deal of information on the economy which had not been available in such handy form since the days of the ill-fated annual Economic Surveys of the late 1940s. The N.E.D.C. report was in two main parts: the first dealing with the Industrial Inquiry, and the second with implications for the economy of a 4 per cent growth rate. The Industrial Inquiry was intended to assess the impact and feasibility for a cross-section of firms in the public and private sectors of a national growth rate of 4 per cent a year. In selecting the industries for investigation, attention was given to the speed at which they would be able to produce the information required, as well as their importance in the economy and the need to cover a reasonable cross-section of British industry including consumer goods, capital goods and service industries in both public and private sectors. At the same time, it was

[1] Sir Ellis Hunter Memorial Lecture, University of York, May 1964.

considered advisable to have in the inquiry industries representing growing points in the economy as well as some which
were in a state of decline. All told the seventeen industries
selected covered about two-fifths of the whole national product
and nearly half of industrial production.[1] The sample included most of the energy industries, some raw materials, for
example steel and chemicals, some capital and some labour
intensive industries, some producing capital goods, some
services and some consumer goods. Looked at in broad terms
there is no doubt that this range of industries could be counted
on to throw up a wide variety of information on different
aspects of growth problems of relevance to the economy as a
whole. It was also considered to have value as a pilot test of the
ability of industries of different kinds, sizes and types, to
respond to a request for information and forecast their future
requirements.

The Industrial Inquiry had the disadvantage, however,
which was also found in the National Plan of 1965, of trying
to bring together in a comparable form material from a great
variety of very different sources. In some cases the trade associations provided the facts and forecasts required, in others
industries made special arrangements for this purpose. The
construction industry established advisory bodies for building
and civil engineering, primarily for liaison with the N.E.D.
Office. In the oil industry there were direct discussions with
six major oil companies. But the general pattern of the inquiry
was for discussion to take place with trade associations,
supplemented where possible and practicable with help from
individual companies, trade unions, Government departments
concerned and anyone else regarded as having special knowledge of particular industries.

Each of the seventeen industries in the inquiry was asked
for:

(a) available statistical information about existing plans
and expectations;

(b) the implications for the industry of an average annual

[1] See *Growth of the United Kingdom Economy to 1966*, H.M.S.O., February
1963.

rate of growth in Gross Domestic Product between 1961–6 of 4 per cent;

(c) information about particular problems that were foreseen as impeding expansion and suggestions for meeting them.

Under the first heading the industries were asked for a forecast of output, exports, imports, employment and capacity on the basis of both present plans and of the 4 per cent case. They were also asked for estimates of gross fixed-capital formation at home for each year from 1961 to 1966, the estimates to be in terms of 1961 prices. Comments were invited on particular points industries might have to make on manpower, training facilities, finance, and research and development trends in their industries. To round the process off views were sought about factors which might affect performance and efficiency, and changes which it was thought might make growth easier.

In order to give a measure of consistency to the information coming in from the inquiry industries were instructed to make their estimates of the impact of the 4 per cent growth rate on a number of common assumptions. These were that the rest of the economy would move forward in the way necessary to achieve a 4 per cent growth rate; that the estimates would relate to individual industries without attempting to take account of the effect of the 4 per cent growth rate over the whole economy on the supply of equipment, materials and manpower to individual industries; that there would be no significant change in the terms of trade between the primary producing countries and manufacturing countries; and that the rate of industrial expansion in the rest of the world would remain at about the same rate as in recent years.

The list of assumptions ended with what, in view of subsequent events, now looks an extremely strange stipulation. This was that Britain could be expected to join the Common Market about halfway through the period, which presumably meant the middle of 1964. It is probable that this assumption appeared in print less as a judgement of possibilities than as a result of the inflexibility of the Government printing arrangements.

This method of collecting information and analysing it to produce an 'industry' view, to support the general forecast and projections on which the programme was based, is open to considerable criticism. In particular, the over-emphasis on consistency is apt to produce a document which has the appearance of reliability but which is in fact only a pale reflection of the truth in economic terms. Mr. Sam Brittan has explained that the popularity of such documents comes from the fact that they appeal to both the politician and the academic planner:

> For the politician a plan that 'adds up' looks a much more convincing document. Economists and statisticians burning the midnight oil to make estimates consistent, are obviously doing a very hard job of work, and not just sounding off their personal opinions or writing ordinary prose which might make politicians or civil servants sceptical of the need for employing them. It would be much more unconventional to bring out an open-ended survey for the next five years, outlining intentions, possibilities and problems, and discussing the alternative ways in which the inconsistencies might be resolved.[1]

This type of inquiry can also be criticised for its reliance on the views of trade associations rather than individual firms. These bodies are best suited to the task of representing specific views on behalf of their industries. When it comes to analysing the broad industrial situation and making forecasts for the years ahead it is inevitable that they should tend to operate in terms of compromise and caution. Like all voluntary bodies they put an excessive value on the opinions of what have been called 'industrial statesmen' who because they seem to be always available, are assumed to be able to speak for their colleagues.

Within the limitations imposed by its terms of reference and organisational framework, the Industrial Inquiry produced an interesting summary of the position and expectation of the industries involved. In fairness it must be said that in the N.E.D. Office the limitations of the results of the Industrial Inquiry were recognised. In the conclusions to Part I of the

[1] 'Inquest on planning in Britain', *Planning*, January 1967.

Growth Programme it was stated, 'it is therefore felt that the estimates can be useful as providing a reasonable picture of how the output of the industries would develop on the growth assumption given, although there are possibilities of substantial errors'.[1] The difficulty is however that estimates contained in a document setting out the national growth programme tend to be taken seriously by the outside world. The members of the Industrial Section of the N.E.D. Office were very conscious of the fact that material had been hastily gathered inside a period of six months, and discounted its value accordingly. They certainly did not see themselves as taking part in what has been called 'a virtuous confidence trick' with the object of persuading businessmen into thinking that faster growth was possible and therefore by their actions bringing it about.

It is a fair summary of the findings of the Industrial Inquiry to say that valuable as they were they had serious limitations.

CONDITIONS FAVOURABLE TO FASTER GROWTH

Although the projections and forecasts of the growth programme were open to considerable criticism, it does not follow that the exercise was not worth while in the situation as it was at that time. The Industrial Inquiry, and discussions and investigations which followed it, produced a great deal of material concerned with obstacles to faster growth. When the N.E.D.C. was set up, one of its objectives was to see what could be done to improve efficiency and whether the best use was being made of resources. This objective was thought of as being separate from the preparation of a forward growth programme. In other words, the Council endeavoured to keep the statement of planning forecasts and policy recommendations separate. It would clearly have been unrealistic, however, for a body on which such high hopes had been placed to content itself with fixing a rate for economic growth and indicating the possible consequences of this for industry and the economy in general, without saying something about the policies needed if the growth programme was to be realised. However, the Council was somewhat reluctant to

[1] *Growth of the United Kingdom Economy to 1966*, para. 115.

produce a policy statement so early in its career. As the weeks went by, following the publication of *Growth of the United Kingdom Economy to 1966*, there was comment in the press on the lack of policy guidance from the Council. There were rumours that a document had been prepared by the Office and was being held back because of disagreements on its publication among Council members. When sections of what were purported to be the N.E.D.C. Policy Statement appeared in the *Guardian* the Council authorised publication. In fact the report had been submitted to the Council by the Director General at its meeting on the 24th January 1963 and was finally authorised for publication on the 5th April.

The report *Conditions Favourable to Faster Growth* has, not surprisingly, worn much better than the Growth Programme itself. It consists of eight sections, each describing a particular problem and its relevance to securing faster growth. The recommendations made were for the most part somewhat diffident and couched in general terms. The problems dealt with were:

- (a) Education and Economic Growth
    Science and technical change
    Management education
    Training
- (b) Mobility and Redundancy
- (c) Regional Questions
- (d) Balance of Payments Policies
- (e) Taxation
- (f) Level of Demand
- (g) Prices and Incomes
- (h) Government, Management and Trade Unions

All the subjects listed are clearly very relevant to securing a faster rate of economic growth. In the period since the publication of the report considerable changes of policy have taken place, some of which were affected by the ideas which were then put forward. For example, the recommendation that there should be 'at least one very high level new school or institute, somewhat on the lines of the Harvard Business School, or the School of Industrial Management at the Massachusetts Institute of Technology' has been acted upon by the establishment of the London and Manchester Business Schools. The analysis of regional questions and the problems concerned with mobility and redundancy have also influenced subsequent policy-making. However, there is no doubt that the reaction to *Conditions Favourable to Faster Growth* was disappointing. Businessmen and politicians who had hoped that the attempt to formulate a plan would result in vigorous public discussion of conditions under which it could operate found this assumption frustrated by political considerations. In particular the expectation that the Government would be forced to make choices between different policy objectives and to establish a firm order of priorities for economic policy proved ill-founded.

To all appearances the N.E.D.C., representing as it did Government, management and trade unions, was an ideal body for the discussion of issues affecting economic policy. Here, if anywhere, the policy-makers and those affected by their actions had a forum in which to reconcile their differences and agree on common courses of action. In the event this did not happen. On the Government side there was a reluctance to give the Council its head as a source of new thinking on subjects for which policies had been formulated and built into election programmes. There were also questions of the constitutional position of an unrepresentative body such as the N.E.D.C. making statements on matters which might be coming up before Parliament. The section on prices and incomes in *Conditions Favourable to Faster Growth* caused considerable comment. It cannot be said, however, that the conclusions drawn were particularly radical. The report said:

There will thus be a need for policies to ensure that money incomes (wages, salaries, profits) as a whole rise substantially less rapidly than in the past. If, however, a growth programme can be achieved, real incomes per head will increase much faster than in the past. They will increase as fast as output per head, or about $3\frac{1}{4}$ per cent a year.

Some of the difficulties experienced in drafting this section of the report were reflected in its final paragraph. This stated that:

A policy for Prices and Incomes can succeed only if those concerned are convinced that it is a necessary part of a wider programme for growth of real incomes, and that restraint by one section of the community will not merely result in a gain by other sections. The Council regards the solution of the difficult problems involved as a necessary part of its task.

A lot of the difficulty experienced by the N.E.D.C. was due to its unique position on the fringe of the administration. Although its purpose was to advise the Chancellor who presided over its meetings, its Office was not part of the Treasury nor indeed of any Government department. It had no executive powers or functions and its chief advantage was, indeed, its independence of the administration. There was nothing in its constitution to prevent the Council publishing reports or issuing statements which were in direct conflict with Government policy. In practice, although discussion in the Council ranged widely, considerable discretion was observed over published statements. The difficulty that might arise if too independent a view was expressed was illustrated in the section on taxation in *Conditions Favourable to Faster Growth*. This contained, in paragraph 170, reference to the hypothetical case of the introduction of a wealth tax in the United Kingdom. The passage read:

A wealth tax in one form or another exists in a good many countries. For example, a Net Personal Wealth Tax has been in operation in Sweden for many years. The introduction of a wealth tax here would be a controversial step but it may have a useful role in any major review of taxation related to a programme for growth.

The fact that this passage was widely quoted as evidence that the N.E.D.C. was advising the Chancellor to introduce a wealth tax had an inhibiting effect on the drafting of future statements for publication. As the Council had to approve everything published by the Office, it is not surprising that its publications have not been remarkable for radical and forthright statements of policy.

The Chancellor of the Exchequer was, in any case, in a difficult position as Chairman of the N.E.D. Council and, at the same time, Minister responsible for economic policy. Because of its constitution, the N.E.D. Office did not have access to the confidential forecasts on the development of the economy produced by the Treasury and other departments. However, this was supposed to be compensated for by the fact that not being bound by Government policy, the Office staff could be much freer in discussing problems and plans with industry and trade unions and in non-Government circles generally. At the same time the Government was clearly involved in the N.E.D.C. operation as a number of senior ministers were members of the Council. Whether this was regarded as a help or a hindrance depended largely on the situation in which the Government found itself at a particular moment. In April 1963 Mr. Reginald Maudling in his first Budget clearly felt himself committed in a general way to the aims of the N.E.D.C. growth policy. He stated: 'The purpose of the Budget . . . is to do the Government's part in achieving the rate of growth . . . which we have already accepted in the National Economic Development Council.' It would, of course, have been difficult for the Chancellor at that point to have taken any other position if the N.E.D.C. growth programme was to be regarded as a framework for Government economic policy. From this point on, however, the political atmosphere changed and it became increasingly difficult for the N.E.D.C. to function satisfactorily. It had never been made clear how far detailed recommendations arising from the growth pro-gramme would be fitted into Government economic policy. These can be divided into those requiring decisions for action at Cabinet level, those where a Minister in a department was required to take action, and those where responsibility rested with industrial management, trade unions or other bodies.

At no stage was there any machinery for ensuring that policy decisions and actions of particular Ministries were consistent

D

with the aims of the N.E.D.C. growth programme. Certainly the Chancellor never had a check list prepared showing the action to be taken under the growth programme by various Ministries, as happened later under the National Plan. In short the N.E.D.C. in its first, or Conservative, phase was overtaken by events. Too new and radical to have established any precedence, too remote from the Establishment to have any political influence or power, it was in the months before the 1964 Election reduced to a state of impotence. Mr. Maudling endeavoured to secure agreement on prices and incomes policies at meetings of the Council in the first part of 1964. However, the certainty that a General Election must be held in October at the latest meant that the trade union and management members were already thinking more about post-election policies and the possibility of a change of Government than the ideas that Mr. Maudling was putting forward. Not only were the discussions in the Council abortive but efforts to increase the number of Economic Development Committees, the Little Neddies, also met with considerable difficulties. By the time of the 1964 Election only nine of these committees consisting of representatives of management, trade unions and independent experts, had been formed. Their function was to act as a connecting link between the Council and their particular industries. But there was little interest in establishing them until the results of the General Election were known.

THE WORK OF THE ECONOMIC DEVELOPMENT COMMITTEES

When the Industrial Inquiry was carried out in 1962 it was realised that the .NE.D.C. would have to have more formal contacts with industry if its forecasts were to be anything more than general indications of what might happen. However, once material for the first green book—*Growth of the United Kingdom Economy*—had been collected, the need to give top priority to speed no longer applied. The Council therefore considered ways and means of establishing more lasting and permanent contacts with industry and at its meeting on the 4th December

1963 approved general arrangements for setting up Economic Development Committees. These had the following terms of reference:

Within the context of the work of the National Economic Development Council and in accordance with such working arrangements as may be determined from time to time, between the Council and the Committee, each Committee will:

(1) examine the economic performance, prospects and plans of the industry and assess from time to time the industry's progress in relation to the national growth objectives, and provide information and forecasts to the Council on these matters;

(2) Consider ways of improving the industry's economic performance, competitive power and efficiency and formulate reports and recommendations on these matters as appropriate.

The first committees were set up during 1963 by the Industrial Division of the N.E.D. Office under Mr. T. C. Fraser. The Division had been actively involved in the collection of the material from industry and as a result of this and the background of its members who had been recruited from industrial firms, it had established working relations with various sectors of industry. It became clear, however, that a small group operating as part of a quasi-independent organisation, such as the N.E.D.C., could not hope to have any lasting influence on management and trade unions. The enthusiasm of the Industrial Division and its desire to exert pressure to focus the attention of industry on the removal of obstacles to growth was unquestioned. The fact that many of those involved had industrial experience and were addressing themselves to former colleagues and acquaintances was all to the good. But trade associations and industrial companies have far too many calls upon their time for them to be able to respond to every circular letter and exhortation that comes their way.

The situation, however, contained grounds for hope. The general attitude within industry towards the work of the National Economic Development Office was favourable. There was a general desire to see an end to stop-go policies and to find the means of achieving faster growth. Many leading

39

industrialists besides the half-dozen involved in the work of the Council were anxious to share in the work of the new organisation. The Trade Union Congress after a somewhat hesitant beginning had become aware of the value of a standing arrangement for joint consultation with Ministers and industrialists covering the whole range of economic and financial problems. The meetings of the Council had provided an opportunity for free and sometimes frank discussion of economic policy at a formative stage, which was quite different from the confrontation which had hitherto taken place in various advisory bodies when Ministers had been mainly concerned to give a preview of their intention at a stage when only minor adjustments might be possible. On the management side the most significant move was the decision to amalgamate the Federation of British Industries, the British Employers' Confederation and the National Union of British Manufacturers. This was not the first attempt to form a single representative industrial body, a task fraught with difficulties.

This new attempt, which led to the formation of the Confederation of British Industry in 1964, owed a great deal of its impetus to the recognition of the need for great coherence of organisation in relation to the work of the National Economic Development Council and Office.

The first moves to set up Economic Development Committees were made in the seventeen industries that had taken part in the Industrial Inquiry for the first growth programme. By the time of the General Election of October 1964 nine E.D.C.s had been set up.

The nine E.D.C.s existing in October 1964

Engineering	Others
Mechanical Engineering	Chemicals
Machine Tools	Wool Textiles
Electrical Engineering	Distribution
Electronics	Paper and Board
	Chocolate and Sugar Confectionery

The instrument for setting up E.D.C.s was the Industrial Division of the N.E.D Office and the principles on which it had worked were not very substantially altered by the change of Government. Perhaps the main difference is that the Department of Economic Affairs now had a predominant say in proposing the industries for which committees should be established and the order in which this should be done. But the process of bringing the parties concerned together remained broadly the same. Each committee consists of representatives of the Government departments concerned, the management organisations and the trade unions, together with some independent members. In some cases the process of sounding out the interests concerned and arriving at a short list of possible members of the E.D.C. may be extremely protracted. The circumstances of different industries vary considerably. In some cases the number of trade unions and trade associations to be consulted will be very considerable. In others one or two strong organisations dominate the industry and the problem is to decide what representation should be given to the smaller bodies involved. If there was such a thing as a typical E.D.C. it would have a chairman, six management representatives, four trade union representatives, one member of the Department of Economic Affairs, one member of the N.E.D. Office, one member of the sponsoring department of the industry (Board of Trade, Ministry of Technology, Ministry of Agriculture, etc.), and at least one independent expert. The process of selection can be very involved. The N.E.D. Office may have a clear idea of who it would like to represent the trade unions or trade associations in any particular industry but it is essential to the working of the system that the parties concerned should have full freedom to put up the names of the representative they want. There is a danger that E.D.C.s will be manned by delegates of particular trade organisations or trade unions bringing closed minds and sectional ideas to the committee meetings. It is perhaps greatest in industries where numbers of organisations have to be consulted in order to decide on a list of half a dozen people acceptable to the score or more of trade associations or trade unions in which the industry is organised. Some of these bodies may be of a splinter character and the fact that they are brought into consultations, and their common interest recognised, helps to secure a sense of involvement in the work of the E.D.C.s throughout the industry.

The most important appointment is that of Chairman. He is selected on the basis of his capacity for leadership and his achievement outside the industry. He must be acceptable to the three parties in the E.D.C., all of which must have their say on the kind of Chairman they want. Whoever is appointed must have wide experience of public affairs and be able to devote time to the business of the Committee. If the representatives of management, trade unions and Government are really to become involved in finding solutions to problems rather than pressing sectional interests, the Chairman must have a complete understanding of the background and history of the matters under discussion. To help the Chairman in his difficult task and to guard against the possibility that he may turn out to be either a 'management' man or a 'trade union' man, provision is made for up to three independent members on the E.D.C.s. Their appointments are also the subject of consultation and it is true to say that in many cases the E.D.C.s have not appointed their full quota of independents. The Chairman is given the principal voice in the selection of independents as they are the element in the Committee best able to provide objective criticism of the views put forward.

The committees are all serviced by the staff of the N.E.D. Office. This also is a matter of importance to the Chairman, as it means that the secretariat owe no special allegiance to any of the main parties concerned. A senior member of the N.E.D. Office serves on each committee as the representative of the Director General. The Committee Secretary is also provided by the N.E.D. Office. Contact between the E.D.C.s and Government departments is maintained in two ways. The Department of Economic Affairs is represented on all E.D.C.s by one of its Industrial Advisers. These are senior men seconded from industry to the department for a two- or three-year period of service. Each of them serves on several E.D.C.s and they are particularly concerned with their contribution to the solution of problems in which the department is especially interested. The fact that their concern is with the performance of the industry in the context of the development of the economy as a whole is another factor in widening the basis of discussion. The other Government representative on the E.D.C.s comes from the sponsor department which has knowledge, responsibility and continuity of concern for the particular industry.

When the scope and composition of an E.D.C. have been settled, and this may have involved talks and discussions with the parties concerned over a period of months, a final meeting is convened by the N.E.D. Office at which all the parties concerned are represented. The invitation to the agreed Chairman is then sent by the Minister of Economic Affairs for the Chairman of the N.E.D.C. (i.e. the Prime Minister). At the same time, the Director General issues invitations to those nominated by the management organisations and the trade unions and to any independent members whose names have been agreed upon at that stage. Invitations are issued to these nominees as individuals and there is no arrangement for trade association or trade unions to send alternates.

The E.D.C. whose formation gave the most difficulty was probably agriculture. This was because both the Ministry of Agriculture and the National Farmers' Union were reluctant to have a body set up which might interfere with the existing organisation of the industry. Not surprisingly, the two parties had no desire to see the annual ritual of the Price Review upset and perhaps superseded by some other arrangement. The trade unions had no part in the Price Review and were therefore much more anxious to see an E.D.C. established for the farming industry in the hope that this would increase their influence on policy-making. In the terms of reference laid down for the E.D.C. the Ministry of Agriculture stipulated that questions dealt with at the Annual Price Review would be outside its scope. The negotiations leading to the setting up of the E.D.C. for Agriculture were extremely protracted, but they serve to illustrate the great importance attached to securing the involvement of the parties concerned. The fact that it was possible to arrive at a workable agreement within the very difficult terms of reference imposed in this and other cases, is a tribute to the patience of the N.E.D. Office staff and particularly to the skill of its Industrial Director, Mr. T. C. Fraser.

The relationship of the E.D.C. to its industry is a somewhat complex one. A member of the E.D.C. begins by accepting the objectives set out in the terms of reference laid down by the Council. He also regards himself in a general sense as a representative of the management or trade union side of his industry. He is therefore aware in all that he says at meetings of the Committee of the general attitudes of his constituents. However, members are not simply delegates, so that each of them in accepting the personal invitation from the Director General to serve on the E.D.C. demonstrates his willingness to take a broad view of the problems of the industry and work with the other members towards finding solutions for them. What is said by a trade union or trade association member at an E.D.C. meeting does not commit his particular organisation but rather reflects the general interests of the industry as he sees them. However, members must be prepared to go back to their constituents and defend recommendations of the E.D.C. to which they have agreed. For example, all E.D.C.s discussed the question of the import/export balance of their industries with special reference to the growing volume of imports of manufactured goods. There is no doubt that many of the recommendations put forward by E.D.C.s on this particular topic would not be wholly acceptable to management or trade unions in certain industries. In these cases it was the duty of the E.D.C. member to argue the case with his constituents in every way possible.

When the first E.D.C.s were being established the main consideration was to secure lines of communication with key industries for the purposes of securing and verifying information needed for the forecasts of economic performance. The rate of progress was not great. Nine E.D.C.s had been set up by October 1964 and twenty by the end of 1965. At that point the major industries were either covered by an E.D.C. or arrangements were in hand to take care of them. The question then arose of the optimum size of the industrial bracket which a committee could be reasonably expected to cover. From the start the object has been to select industries which provided a cross-section both in type of product and in size for the economy as a whole. The object was to cover as much of industry as possible with the smallest number of E.D.C.s, in other words, to set up committees covering as large a sector as possible. The effect of this has been that E.D.C. members have usually been called upon to deal with problems in a wider context than the one to which they are generally used. It is of course easier to deal with the smaller and more integrated industries in this way than with those covering a wider range of activities. Apart from anything else, where a committee covers too wide a span the lines of communication between management and trade union representatives and the industry becomes extremely tenuous. There is more likelihood in arriving at conclusions which have meaning and to which members are committed when they are drawn from only two or three organisations to which they can directly and effectively make their views known to a reasonably comprehensive membership, than when they have to make contact through a network of ten or twenty organisations. There is clearly a limit to the number of sectors of the economy that can be effectively covered by Economic Development Committees. The difficulties that arise in industries organised on a very diffuse pattern are illustrated by building and construction. Two E.D.C.s have been set up, one covering building, the other civil engineering. The problem of how to co-ordinate their activities has been solved by appointing the same chairman for both committees. The only nationalised industry covered by an E.D.C. is the Post Office. This Committee first met on the 14th March 1966.

A list of E.D.C.s is given in Appendix III.

E.D.C.S AND ECONOMIC POLICY

E.D.C.s are expected to play a significant part in the formulation and implementation of economic policy. It is clearly important therefore that ways and means should be found of using the ideas and views put forward by E.D.C.s to influence Government policy-making, and supplying information on which policy decisions can be based. At the same time the

E.D.C.s are operating as a link between national objectives for public purposes and private enterprise and private decision-making. It is extremely difficult to assess how far decision-making of individual firms will take account of views expressed by E.D.C.s, but there is no doubt that certain general questions of policy discussed by the E.D.C.s can be very important indeed. The great problem is how to co-ordinate the activities of the various parts of the machinery which has been set up for integrating economic policy-making and carrying out its general objectives. The Economic Development Committees operating within the N.E.D. Office have direct links through the Director General with the Council and also with the Department of Economic Affairs. At organisational level there are links with the D.E.A. through the membership of its Industrial Advisers on the E.D.C.s. There are less direct contacts with other departments, such as the Board of Trade and Ministry of Technology, which are the sponsors of particular industries.

One criticism of the present arrangements which has been voiced from time to time is that the E.D.C.s have no close contact with the work of the Council. From the beginning it has been the convention that no Chairman of an E.D.C. could also be a member of Council. From time to time the Council has had on its Agenda a report from the Chairman of an E.D.C. on the work of his committee. In some cases this gesture has done more harm than good as the Chairman concerned having prepared a report has found that other business has taken so long that discussion of his E.D.C. was rushed through in a brief time before lunch. This lack of contact between E.D.C. chairmen and Council members can lead to frustration on both sides. One suggestion that has been put forward is that two E.D.C. chairmen should serve as members of the Council for a fixed term in rotation. One difficulty with such an arrangement is that there is no formal machinery by which the two representatives could report back to the rest of the E.D.C. chairmen. Another possibility is that the Industrial Director of the N.E.D. Office should be made a member of Council. This would enable him to take part in discussions on the work of the E.D.C.s.

The great value of the E.D.C.s lies in the fact that they represent a voluntary commitment by people of considerable influence in the industries concerned. The benefit of this commitment can be lost if the operation becomes over-organised so that more independent industrialists no longer find membership attractive. Only if E.D.C.s are really in a position to influence policy decisions can they be regarded as useful and effective parts of the machinery of Government. It is fundamental to the idea of the E.D.C.s that the members should have a sense of shared responsibility for both planning and efficiency. The industrial representatives are under an obligation to blend their responsibility to their constituents with an overall concern for the contribution of their industry to the national objectives. The grouping of the E.D.C.s within the N.E.D. Office, serviced by a single staff, ensures that the priorities of work of planning and efficiency of the whole range of industries are synchronised. Within the Office there are links between the staff members dealing with different industries and it is possible to make cross-references regarding the impact of specific problems. If this network of E.D.C.s is to operate successfully, it is essential that it should be adequately staffed. There have been complaints that senior members of the N.E.D. Office staff have had too many E.D.C.s to supervise. Another complaint is that the N.E.D. Office representative on some E.D.C.s have not always been of the right level of seniority. While there is no doubt that if the same man is looking after four E.D.C.s he has a fair idea of what is going on in each, he will at the same time have difficulty in keeping up with the background reading and making the contacts in industry, the universities and elsewhere which he should be doing if he is to do justice to his assignment. Another problem is the very rapid rate of turnover of N.E.D. Office staff. Those coming from industry usually do so on a two-year secondment which by any standards is a somewhat brief period in which to come to grips with the problems of a number of industries.

Although it is perhaps too soon to pronounce a verdict on the E.D.C.s, there is no doubt that they may prove to be one of the most useful institutional innovations of the last decade. The fact that they were used as instruments for the collection of information for the forecasts and projections of the original growth programme and later of the National Plan has tended to obscure the fact that their most effective role is as forums for discussion of specific problems. The shelving of the National Plan after the introduction of the Government's deflationary measures on 20th July 1966 gave the E.D.C.s a new lease of life. The work which they have done since that time has been devoted to questions where, because of their unique composition, they have been able to make a real contribution to better understanding. The trend has in fact been back towards the kind of discussion on which the N.E.D. Council was engaged in 1963 and which resulted in the 'Orange Book'—*Conditions Favourable to Faster Growth*. There is no doubt that this movement is very much to the liking of industrial managers and trade unionists who give so much of their time to E.D.C. work. Freed from the sophistries of target-making, the E.D.C.s should be able to get down to the task about which their members know more than anyone else in the country, that is, how to govern their own industries.

IV
Government Organisations and Industry

Criticisms of the handling of economic policy by the Treasury became general in the early 1960s but had been heard in more specialised circles long before.[1] The complaint most often heard was that the Treasury invariably put the needs of sterling first, and that the growth of the domestic economy was being stunted by the policy of deflating it whenever the balance of payments showed signs of getting into difficulties. The decision to set up the Department of Economic Affairs was regarded by many critics of the Treasury as a new and exciting departure. D.E.A.'s function according to the first issue of its *Progress Report* (January 1965), was responsibility for 'the long-term aspects of economic policy and its first concern is with physical resources'.

The change in the direction of the economy that has taken place since 1964 is shown in the operation of the existing and new Ministries now concerned with economic and commercial policy. The main element in the change was the reduction of the importance of the Treasury and of what it used to do, namely, control the expansion of the economy through the management of demand. The emphasis shifted to the stimulation of the flow of goods and resources by removing bottlenecks to productive efficiency, giving incentives to export, subsidising businesses going to the Development Areas and in these and other ways controlling the supply side of the economy. A whole host of bodies, some efficient, some inexperienced, with no

[1] For example, *Growth in the British Economy*, P.E.P., 1960; *The British Economy since the War*, Andrew Shonfield, Penguin, 1958.

executive powers began working away alongside the Government economic departments. Whatever else can be said of economic policy, industrialists cannot complain of being neglected. The devaluation of the pound in November 1967 represented a swing back to Treasury control of the economy, although the various policies begun by the D.E.A. are likely to continue.

The departments which most closely concern industry in its day to day activities are the Treasury, the Board of Trade and the Department of Economic Affairs and the Ministry of Technology. Each of these in one way or another exerts considerable influence on the way companies operate. In addition, the Ministry of Labour[1] and the Ministry of Transport affect the resources available and the way in which they are used. A number of other departments, the Ministry of Defence, the Ministry of Housing, the Ministry of Agriculture, affect particular industries either as purchasers of products or through controlling the scale of remuneration of their producers.

THE TREASURY

Most companies are affected by the financial and economic work of the Treasury either directly through taxation or exchange-control policy, or indirectly through its control of public expenditure and general short-term regulation of the economy. For the most part the Treasury does not have as much direct contact with individual companies as some other departments. Of the matters of most concern to industry, exchange control questions are normally dealt with by the Bank of England while taxation is the concern of the Inland Revenue and Customs and Excise. The Capital Issues Committee which has a considerable influence on investment is a part of the Treasury. Formerly the Chancellor of the Exchequer was in charge of both long- and-short term economic policy. However, his position has changed since the reorganisation carried out as a result of the work of the Plowden Committee in 1962. This was not in any way connected with the setting up of the National Economic Development Council and followed on

[1] Its name was changed to Ministry of Employment and Productivity in April 1968.

from a process dating back to 1957. Criticism of the Treasury control over spending of other Government departments by the Select Committee on Estimates resulted in the appointment of a Special Committee under Lord Plowden, consisting of five people from inside the civil service and three from outside. Its report was published in 1961 as a White Paper.[1] The original Plowden Report was a confidential document submitted to the Chancellor of the Exchequer. The published version identified two major deficiencies in the existing system. First it said that decisions about Government expenditure were taken on an *ad hoc* basis without any specific reference to likely public needs or to the future resources available to meet them. The report added that there was no adequate machinery for bringing competing demands of the different departments of Government together in a single coherent picture which would enable the Cabinet to decide on the orders of priority of Government spending.

The resulting re-organisation had the effect of recasting the entire structure of the Treasury. Previously one Permanent Secretary had been in charge of the Treasury with two Joint Permanent Secretaries, one responsible for the co-ordination of economic policy and the control of public expenditure, and the other for the management of the civil service and of some other parts of the public services. In addition the holder of this post was also Secretary of the Cabinet. The Plowden Committee decided that the management functions of the Treasury had been expanding and would develop further. It was decided therefore that the Joint Permanent Secretary in charge of the civil service should be freed of other major responsibilities outside the Treasury, and the post of Secretary of the Treasury was detached from this work.

Under the new system the Treasury was organised on a more functional basis which lent itself more readily to broader methods of financial control based on long-term forecasts of resources and expenditure which were being increasingly used in the Treasury. The new arrangement was also much more in line with modern concepts of management.

[1] *Control of Public Expenditure*, H.M.S.O., Cmnd. 1432.

Functionally the Treasury is now divided into four groups: the Pay Group, which deals with pay and working conditions of the various classes of civil servants and with questions on the pay of staffs in other parts of the public service; the Management Group, responsible for developing management services, whose activities include organisation and methods work, inquiries into and comparisons of management practices over a wide field, and the work of recruitment, training, manning and grading in the civil service; the Finance Group, which brings together all questions affecting home and overseas finance; and the fourth group concerned with balancing public expenditure against national resources and organising the control of this expenditure under such broad headings as Defence, Social Services, Agriculture and Transport.

The reorganisation within the Treasury is of considerable significance in view of what has happened since the change of Government. Although the coincidence in timing between it and the establishment of the N.E.D.C. was largely fortuitous, the fact that they took place together does mean that a complete organisational structure for economic planning was created. The setting up of the Department of Economic Affairs was in fact less revolutionary than was generally thought and consisted essentially of a rearrangement of existing units within the organisation.

So far as companies are concerned the impact of the work of the Treasury is most noticeable in its dealings with the balance of payments, the strength of sterling, and problems of inflation. Periodic balance of payments crises have occurred when payments both visible and invisible have exceeded receipts. In these cases the Treasury has acted to check the level of activity in the economy by introducing a 'squeeze' which operates through checks on hire purchase sales principally on consumer durables such as motor cars, motor cycles, refrigerators and domestic appliances. Restrictions imposed usually affect the down payment and the period of repayment of the sums involved. The Treasury also has power to use what is called the economic regulator which enables a surcharge of 10 per cent to be imposed on the duties on beer, wines and spirits, on hydrocarbon oils, petrol substitutes and methylated spirit, and on Purchase Tax without any special legislation being necessary.

The main control of the Treasury over expenditure is, of course, exercised through the Annual Budget, which is normally the main occasion of the year for reviewing the Exchequer finances and the economic state of the nation. In his Budget speech the Chancellor estimates the yield of the Revenue on the basis of existing taxation and proposes the changes that he considers desirable on economic grounds in order to meet the estimates of expenditure for the coming year. These proposals are later embodied in detail in a Finance Bill.

TAXATION EFFECTS

The raising of taxation is much more than a purely financial operation. It affects the distribution of income and property, the level of expenditure on particular kinds of goods and services. Also the general level of taxation affects the degree of activity of the economy as a whole, a matter which is of considerable importance to industry. Over the last twenty years Budgets have been consciously designed to bring the total demand for goods and services into balance with supplies which it is estimated could be made available. The main instrument available to the Chancellor is the taxation of income and capital at varying rates through income tax and surtax, and through company taxation. Taxes on expenditure such as those on drink and tobacco do not affect the distribution of income and their main purpose has always been the raising of revenue. However, by discouraging or encouraging consumption of particular goods, taxation can be used to influence the allocation of resources and the pattern of trade. For the businessman the operations of the Treasury at this level mean that money is scarce so that people have less to spend on his products or that demand is likely to rise because the Chancellor begins to get worried about the number of people unemployed. A lot depends however on the Government's own expenditure. If public spending on the social services, education, defence, goes up without any increase in taxation, then there is more money to spend and the total demand for goods and services rises. This

E

can also mean, of course, that employment goes up. If, however, taxation is increased without any rise in Government spending, then the total demand for goods and services will fall. The businessman may therefore find that the Chancellor, by varying the amount of money available, is having a considerable effect on the demand for his products. In recent years the aim of the 1961 Budget was to counter inflation and to encourage exports; this was done by higher taxation. The following year it was decided that the process of cutting back had gone far enough and taxation was eased. In 1963 and 1964 the Government had adopted the objective of a 4 per cent growth rate so that expansionary Budgets were introduced. In the next two years the main problem was the Balance of Payments deficit so the Budgets of 1965 and 1966 had been aimed at reducing the net outflow of long-term capital through the regulation of overseas investment and the changes in company taxation and cutting down the level of activity in the economy in order to check imports. The 1966 Budget also attempted a new type of regulation of the economy through the introduction of the Selective Employment Tax which was aimed at encouraging long-term structural changes in the economy.

Taxes levied in the United Kingdom fall into three main categories. These are taxes on income, including Income Tax, Surtax and Corporation Tax; taxes on capital, including Estate Duty, Capital Gains Tax and the tax on short-term gains; and taxes on expenditure, including Customs and Excise duties, Purchase Tax, Selective Employment Tax (on services), local rates, stamp duties, licence duties on motor vehicles, etc. The Board of Inland Revenue collects taxes on income and capital while the Board of Customs and Excise collects those on expenditure, including Purchase Tax. There are a number of other authorities responsible for the collection of the remainder, including the Ministry of Social Security which collects the Selective Employment Tax. This tax, which has been widely criticised, was intended to discourage the use of labour in the service industries. It became operative in September 1966. It is paid by all employers throughout the

United Kingdom at a rate per week of 25s. for men, 12s. 6d. for women and boys, and 8s. for girls. Employers are affected by the tax in various ways. Those in manufacturing industry receive a refund of tax and a premium which together amount to 32s. 6d. for men, 16s. 3d. for women and boys, and 10s. 6d. for girls. Employers in transport, public services, including the nationalised industries, agriculture, extractive industries and charities have the tax refunded but receive no premium, while employers in the service industries and in construction pay the tax without any refund whatsoever. The Selective Employment Tax is the most obvious example in recent years of the attempt to influence the policies of businessmen through the tax system.

The work of the Treasury also comes into the open through changes in the Bank Rate. This is the rate at which the Bank of England discount approved Bills of Exchange and it is a key factor in deciding the general pattern of interest rates. The raising or lowering of the Bank Rate is the main instrument in the Government's monetary policy. If the Chancellor believes that industry is embarking on too many new schemes and that too much money is being borrowed from the Banks, he will raise the rate to make this more difficult. If, on the other hand, he wants to stimulate investment the Bank Rate will come down. This means that a businessman may find himself in a position where his company needs to raise money for expansion at the very moment when because of the balance of payments position or for some other reason affecting the working of the economy as a whole, the Chancellor increases the Bank Rate and puts a check on all borrowing whatever its motives.

The other way in which the Bank of England most closely affects the activities of businessmen is through its role as the Government's agent for the administration of exchange control which determines the movement of money in and out of the country.

THE DEPARTMENT OF ECONOMIC AFFAIRS

The Department of Economic Affairs was set up in October 1964 by the Labour Government. It was headed by the First Secretary of State and Secretary of State for Economic Affairs, but the first part of this title has since been transferred to the reconstituted Ministry of Labour. The Ministry does not have detailed executive functions, its principal concern is with the planning and co-ordination of economic policy including the efficient use of physical resources over the longer term. Short-term measures to regulate the economy and the balance of payments are dealt with by the Treasury, but as these can affect long-term plans and long-term policy may have short-term implications, the D.E.A. and the Treasury necessarily have to work in close co-operation.

The department was originally organised in four main interrelated groups:

The General Planning Group is responsible for forecasts and projections of the course of the economy over all but the short-term period and carries out detailed work on particular industries. In this connection, as on the occasion of the preparation of the National Plan, businessmen may be asked to provide information on their future plans, export prospects and so on. This group undertakes and commissions a considerable amount of research into key economic problems as well as being closely concerned with development of techniques of economic projections for the purpose of forecasting the growth and changing pattern of the economy.

The Industrial Prices and Incomes Group is responsible for industrial policy and for prices and incomes policy. This group has a number of Industrial Advisers who are senior industrialists seconded to the D.E.A. for a period. They represent the D.E.A. on the Economic Development Committees (Little Neddies) for individual industries. The section of the group dealing with prices and incomes policy which works closely with the Prices and Incomes Board has been transferred to the Ministry of Employment and Productivity.

The Regional Planning Group is responsible for regional aspects of national policies on industry, employment, land use and transport and for inter-departmental co-ordination in this field. Here again businessmen may find themselves called upon to supply information to the Economic Planning Board in their region.

The External Policies Group was responsible for co-ordinating the views of different Government departments on international economic issues. In particular this group has examined the economic implications of membership of the European Economic Community. This function and other matters concerning international trade, defence, and other overseas expenditure, aid to the developing countries, export credit and similar matters are now carried out by the Treasury.

The principal contacts of the D.E.A. with industry come through the Economic Development Committees set up by the National Economic Development Council. The N.E.D. Council was formerly under the chairmanship of the Secretary of State for Economic Affairs, but the Prime Minister has presided since he took over responsibility for economic policy in August 1967. The members include the President of the Board of Trade, the Minister of Technology, the First Secretary of State and Minister for Employment and Productivity, representatives of management and of the trade unions. The Economic Development Committees so far appointed cover about two-thirds of private industry, while the Post Office is the first to be covered in the public sector. The E.D.C.s examine problems in their industries such as the need for rationalisation, the slow rate of growth of exports, the inefficient use of labour and so on. As many of the E.D.C.s have set up Working Parties and sub-committees, the number of businessmen involved in their activities is very considerable. The E.D.C.s played a considerable part in the preparation of the National Plan and will no doubt do so again in any similar exercise in the future.

As part of the Government changes which took place on 28th August 1967, the Prime Minister assumed responsibility for the Department of Economic Affairs with the Secretary of State for Economic Affairs and other Ministers in the department working under his general direction. This arrangement came to an end in April 1968.

The main object of the new structure for the co-ordination of economic policy was to provide a consistent and constant long-term strategy for securing the growth of the economy. This need can be stated simply, perhaps too simply, as the necessity

57

for preventing decisions by the Treasury for the control of expenditure or the regulation of the level of demand to the balance of payments, from taking precedence over long-term policy. Reconciling these different requirements and time scales is extremely difficult as the fate of the National Plan has demonstrated. It is not possible to subordinate short-term policy to long-term requirements but there is some room for manœuvre and some choices are available for short-term policy that affect the development of the economy over longer periods. If there is no consistent system for long-term objectives then economic policy is always in danger of becoming a hotchpotch of short-term expedients. In other words, economic planning must be a matter of reconciling the short- and long-term needs of the situation in order to arrive at a set of policies which together make up a credible strategy for the achievement of stated objectives.

The Department of Economic Affairs was for a time the centre of an increasing network of associated and subordinate bodies concerned with different aspects of the running of the economy. Some of these were already in existence and were taken over and developed, for example, the N.E.D.C. and its Economic Development Committees. Others were set up especially to perform definite tasks. Of these the Prices and Incomes Board and the Industrial Reorganisation Corporation are the most important. Farther afield there are the Regional Economic Development Boards and Councils which together are responsible for the regional aspects of the D.E.A.'s work.

THE MINISTRY OF TECHNOLOGY

The Ministry of Technology (Mintech) was also created in October 1964. Its task was defined as being to 'guide and stimulate a major national effort to bring advanced technology and new processes into British industry'. It became the sponsoring department for four industries: computers, machine tools, electronics and telecommunications, all chosen because of their special relevance to the objectives of the Ministry. Since then its sponsorship has been extended until it now covers virtually the whole of the electrical, electronic and mechanical engineering industries, including electrical and mechanical engineering products generally, motor vehicles, electrical and process plant, aircraft and aero engines and shipbuilding. It has also acquired responsibility for engineering standards and weights and measures and for the British Standards Institution. Other duties and responsibilities which the Ministry has taken over include most of the functions of the Department of Scientific Research, including the National Physical Laboratory and the National Engineering Laboratory and also responsibility for the National Research Development Corporation and for the United Kingdom Atomic Energy Authority.

The question of sponsorship of an industry by a Government department is one of considerable importance. It means that the main point of contact for the industry with the Government machine is through this department. It is a contact which is distinct from the miscellaneous transactions with individual Government departments in which companies directly, or through their trade associations, find themselves involved. The relationship is of a positive nature involving examination of the problems of particular industries in order to identify measures which Government can take in collaboration with industry to help solve these problems. As part of this function the Ministry of Technology has taken over the responsibilities of the former Ministry of Aviation with regard to meeting the Defence Ministry's requirements for aircraft and airborne weapons and equipment, guided missiles and nuclear weapons and the greater part of the military requirements for radio, radar and other electronic equipment. The Ministry is also involved in carrying out and encouraging measures for the design, development and production of civil aircraft and of the electronic equipment required for civil aircraft and air-traffic control. The research and development resources of the Royal Aircraft Establishment and the Royal Radar Establishment, formerly under the Ministry of Aviation, and also the former D.S.I.A. stations, are now under Mintech control.

The impact of Mintech on industry is felt in a variety of ways. Those industries which it sponsors have direct relationship with it through its work of research and development, for

59

example, in machine tools, or the schemes for rationalisation to be carried out by the Shipbuilding Industry Board. Other industries can make use of various facilities which are now available through the Ministry. The National Computing Centre set up in July 1966 to standardise and simplify the programming of computers and to advise on the training of systems analysts and programmers is used by firms from a wide range of industries. Companies using machine tools may wish to take advantage of the scheme introduced to shorten the gap between development of advanced machine tools and their adoption by users. For this purpose the Ministry has instituted a 'pre-production order' scheme in which the Ministry is prepared to buy advanced models and place them out on free loan for initial valuation and trial by potential purchasers. The advantage of this scheme to the purchaser is that he is able to try out a new machine without having to bear an undue risk.

In some cases, as for example electronics, the Ministry is itself a major purchaser of the products of the industry, and a pace setter in the use of the most technologically advanced products. In the capital goods sector some 40 per cent of the electronics industry's output is for defence requirements, and the bulk of the research and development financed by the government now takes place in the Ministry's own research establishments and through its contacts with industry and the universities. In this connection the Ministry has important opportunities for exploiting the fall-out from military research work for civil applications.

Outside the range of its sponsored industries, the main activity of the Ministry lies in the mobilisation and deployment of its research and development resources. In its various establishments it has a total qualified manpower of about 9,000 persons. Although a substantial volume of the work is on behalf of other Government departments, the research establishments are increasingly emphasising the importance of their work for the needs of industry. Apart from the major research establishments and research stations, there are some forty-five research associations which are autonomous co-operative industrial organisations controlled by their members but which are grant-aided and operate under the aegis of the Ministry. These cater for about 55 per cent of British industry on a turnover basis and their total income is about £40 million. The total membership of the Research Associations is about 19,000, which includes multi-memberships for certain large firms of varied interests. Five research establishments obtain the bulk of their industrial income by statutory levy, these are cotton, wool, cast iron, furniture and cutlery. Outstanding examples of recent achievements by such establishments are the spray steel process developed by the British Iron and Steel Research Association and now taken up by a number of firms. Another is the baking process for synthetic yarns by the Linen Research Association and a quick bread-making process by the Flour Milling and Baking Research Association.

The role of technology in improving productivity generally is one with which businessmen are familiar. The Ministry is working in this field through its Industrial Operations Unit which demonstrates the effectiveness of modern management methods and techniques by investigating problems of interest to a wide cross-section of industry. Regional offices which draw on the resources of the Ministry, the universities and the research associations, all help local industry directly. The Ministry also provides a Production Engineering Advisory Service which is organised regionally.

THE BOARD OF TRADE

The Board of Trade is a very large and in many ways old-fashioned department which has a general responsibility in respect of the United Kingdom's commerce, industry and overseas trade, including commercial relations with other countries, imports and trade, the protective tariff, industrial development and consumer protection. In addition, it is responsible for (1) the promotion of exports, (2) statistics of trade and industry both home and abroad, including the census of production and distribution, and (3) administration of certain legislation, for example, in relation to patents, registered designs, copyright, trade marks, weights and measures,

61

merchandise marks, companies, bankruptcy, insurance, shipping, distribution of industry, films and enemy property.

The activities of the Board of Trade have been reduced by the taking over of regional policy by the D.E.A. and of the sponsorship of a number of industries, already described, by Mintech. All the same it is still an extremely important part of the economic policy machinery. Its principal activities are the stimulation of exports, the publication of monthly trade figures, registration of companies, the distribution of industry and the administration of the cash grants and other incentives to companies setting up in the Development Areas. The Board has a number of independent corporate bodies and other organisations working with it on specific problems. These include the British National Export Council, the British Productivity Council, the Council of Industrial Design, the Monopolies Commission and the Consumer Council.

Between them the Treasury, D.E.A., Mintech and the Board of Trade cover the main elements of economic policy and industrial development. The changes that have taken place since October 1964 have resulted in responsibility for industry being spread over the D.E.A., Mintech and the Board of Trade. This has not made for efficiency and there is no doubt that further rationalisation will be necessary. The form that this might take is discussed in Chapter IX.

THE MINISTRY OF EMPLOYMENT AND PRODUCTIVITY

A number of other Ministries affect the operation of industry. The Ministry of Employment and Productivity operates with other departments on matters of general employment policy, including the distribution of industry, the maintenance of a high and steady rate of employment and research into medium- and long-term trends in the distribution of manpower between industries and occupations. In the reallocation of functions in April 1968 the Ministry was renamed and took over responsibility for the Prices and Incomes Policy. The Ministry provides a national system of employment exchanges which includes a Professional and Executive Register at thirty-nine of the larger Exchanges. It also operates Government schemes for vocational training and industrial rehabilitation, administers the Youth Employment Service, and provides the Disablement Resettlement Service which helps disabled persons find work.

Other functions of the department include the resettlement in civilian employment of men released from the Armed Forces, the supervision through the Factory Inspectorate, of safety, health and welfare measures for workers in industry and commerce, the provision of services for conciliation, arbitration and investigation in industrial disputes, responsibility for questions arising from the administration of the Wages Council Act of 1959, and the collection and publication of labour statistics of all kinds.

Of particular interest to business is the administration of the Industrial Training Act which is carried out by the department. Under this Act provision was made for the setting up of Industrial Training Boards for individual industries, each consisting of a chairman from industry with an equal number of employer and trade union members and a number of educational members. The Act covers all activities of industry and commerce and the intention is that every industry will eventually come within the scope of the Training Board. Employers are bound to pay a levy at a scale determined by the Board for their industry and will receive grants in respect of approved training which they carry out. It is not possible for employers to challenge the rate of levy which the Board has proposed but they can challenge the assessment, for example, on the grounds that a company is not liable to pay a levy to that particular Board or that the assessment has not been accurately calculated.

THE MINISTRY OF HOUSING AND LOCAL GOVERNMENT

Although this Ministry is mainly concerned with housing, and the national housing programme, some of its powers affect industry. In particular the development of land, sewerage and other services come within its sphere. Businessmen concerned over the development of land which they own or be about to acquire may be in contact with the Ministry over questions of planning permission. The designation of new towns and their

Development Corporations is also the responsibility of the Ministry.

THE MINISTRY OF POWER

The business of producing and distributing gas, electricity and the production of coal is operated by the Boards of the three nationalised industries which are responsible to the Ministry on policy issues. Government relations with the petroleum industry are also within the sphere of this department. Companies owning or proposing to construct pipelines come under the regulations imposed by the Ministry of Power. Also it is specifically responsible for the use of atomic energy as a source of industrial power and for the safety of nuclear installations other than those operated by the U.K. Atomic Energy Authority. The Ministry is also responsible for the legislation governing the safety and health of workers in coal mines, metalliferous mines and quarries.

THE HOME OFFICE

The Home Office is responsible for certain technical and legal regulations applying to industry. Broadly speaking, the Home Office is entrusted with all the responsibilities of national administration which have not been specially assigned by law or convention to another Minister. Among these are the regulation of the employment of children and young persons, immigration control and naturalisation of aliens, granting licences for scientific experiments on animals, supervising the control of explosives, firearms and dangerous drugs, and responsibility for Civil Defence and the Fire Service.

The Home Office is in manufacturing in a small way as it is responsible for the administration of the State Management Scheme for control of the liquor trade in the Carlisle district, which places a brewery and 175 licensed premises under its charge.

THE MINISTRY OF AGRICULTURE, FISHERIES AND FOOD

Industry is most affected by the regulations covering food

manufacture and processing. These include a number of technical regulations concerning labelling and advertising of food products, questions relating to the supply and manufacture of food, its consumption, preservation and nutritional qualities. The Ministry maintains a comprehensive information service and gives free technical advice.

DIRECTION OF ECONOMIC POLICY

In recent years the contacts between Government departments and industry have increased considerably. Departments are the main instruments for giving effect to Government policy when Parliament has passed the necessary legislation. The way in which they do this varies according to what is involved. In some cases they act through local authorities, in others through Statutory Boards, or Government-sponsored organisations. Contacts between company directors and Government departments occur either directly or through membership of trade association committees, or any one of the host of working parties and committees which have been set up as a means of discussing, implementing and in some cases formulating economic policy. A change of Government does not necessarily affect the number or general functions of Government departments, although, as happened in 1964, the policy implications of changes that may take place on the entry into power of a new Government can be very far-reaching indeed. The same is true of changes due to the re-allocation of duties between departments which since August 1967 have shifted power and influence from the D.E.A. back towards the Treasury and the grandly titled Ministry of Employment and Productivity.

V
The National Plan

The National Plan was published on the 14th September 1965 and was effectively strangled on the 20th July 1966 when the Government introduced a number of severe deflationary measures in the hope of ending the series of sterling crises. The preparation of such a plan had been an integral part of the reorganisation of the machinery for economic policy-making and control introduced after the 1964 Election. In the opening words of the foreword Mr. George Brown, First Secretary of State, said: 'The publication by the Government of a plan covering all aspects of the country's economic development in the next five years is a major advance in economic policy-making.'

He went on to say that the Plan had been prepared in the fullest consultation with industry and represented 'a statement of Government policy and a commitment to action by the Government'. The First Secretary also warned that the most serious economic problem facing Britain at that time was the balance of payments and the need to eliminate the deficit and repay the debts incurred in financing past deficits. To do this, exports must be increased which meant greater efficiency and competitiveness in industry. The Plan, he claimed, set out the policies and the actions needed to achieve these ends. The Plan was also described as a 'Guide to action'. To this end the Government was discussing with industry the measures needed to implement the Plan. 'Leaders in management and the trade unions', it was stated, 'have a special responsibility, but it cannot be left solely to them.' Finally, the First Secretary stated that to make the Plan work required above all an acceptance of change. 'For the manufacturer, changes in what he makes, what he sells, and where he sells it; for the worker, changes in what he does, where he does it, and how he does it; and for all of us a different approach to prices and incomes.'

The National Plan had been seen in various stages during its preparation by the National Economic Development Council. At one time it had been suggested that an outline plan should be published as a sort of trailer for the main document. The members of the Council were by no means unanimous in their enthusiasm for the Plan. This feeling was reflected in a note which appeared at the beginning of the Plan stating that it had been considered in draft at the meeting of the N.E.D.C. under the chairmanship of Mr. Brown on the 5th August. Except for minor alterations, this was in fact the final draft of the Plan which had been prepared as a result of the frantic efforts of the staff of the D.E.A. and the N.E.D. Office. The statement agreed by the Council for publication at the beginning of the National Plan was in extremely cautious terms. It accepted it as 'a valuable analysis of the problems to be overcome in achieving a growth in the National Product of 25 per cent between 1964 and 1970, acknowledged the "vital part" which the Council and the Economic Development Committees would have to play in overcoming the obstacles to growth, and ended by emphasising the crucial nature of the balance of payments problem'.

Before examining the Plan, there are one or two observations to be made which have a bearing on its rise and fall. On the political side it was inevitable that a Labour Government would have to attempt to improve on the Conservative version of planning exemplified by the N.E.D.C. The propaganda in favour of 'planning with teeth' and planning by people who 'believe in planning' was an understandable political reaction to what was regarded by many Socialists as an attempt by the Conservatives to steal their policies. It was inevitable also that the changes in the Government machinery should influence the type of Plan produced. The emphasis in the N.E.D.C. Growth Programme had been on the formulation of the agenda for economic policy which was credible to management and trade unions and accepted by Government. The National Plan was characterised by machinery rather than policies. It was a means of carrying forward a rationalisation of economic policy and providing it with the central direction. A development of this kind was predictable. 'If the ends of Government are to be more specific, then sometimes the means must be also.'[1]

The lack of precision about the place of the N.E.D.C. in the administrative machine had always been a source of weakness, raising political and constitutional questions. But so was the question which is still very much open to argument, of whether the main source of our difficulties lies in a lack of understanding of how the economic system works or in the failure of successive Governments to put across the reasons for their economic policies. There is also the question of confidence in any Government's ability to carry out its policies or adopt measures appropriate to the situation. This presupposes that the policy-makers have economic wisdom on their side and that all that is needed is that managers, trade unionists and the public at large should have the common sense to appreciate what is being done for them. The opposite view is that the policy-makers and Government officials do not themselves understand the situation and are therefore putting forward policies based on an incorrect analysis. It is this second possibility which constitutes the principal argument for having an organisation such as the N.E.D. Office containing professional economists who are somewhat detached from day-to-day problems and have not acquired a departmental view and attitudes. These people would have an opportunity of working out what Sir Roy Harrod[2] has called the 'new applied economics' through being brought up against practical problems as they impinge on Government policies. Whether this would or not have come about is difficult to say in view of the rather short time that the N.E.D. Office was in existence in its original independent form. In any event, both the acceptance of the growth objective

[1] *Bureaucracy or Management?* An Inaugural Lecture by Peter Self, L.S.E. and G. Bell & Sons, January 1965.

[2] Sir Roy Harrod, *The Times Review of Industry*, June 1964.

and of the N.E.D.C. as the means of bringing it about were still far from complete at the time of the 1964 Election. The lack of progress during the months before the General Election had made it clear that if the purpose of planning is to see that something happens other than what would have happened without it, then the N.E.D.C. was an imperfect instrument.

The National Plan when it appeared eleven months after the Election bore all the marks of hasty production. It was a mixture of forecast, feasibility study, policy directive, industrial targetry and a dissertation on the economic facts of life. Because of the short time available for its preparation its presentation left a great deal to be desired. The impression was not that the Government had made a careful review of all the factors involved and arrived at policy decisions as a result of this, but that a mass of material had been gathered in the hope that directives would emerge from the study of it. The best that can be said of the Plan is that it was very good considering the speed at which it was produced. The Plan was variously described as a 'Statement of Government Policy', 'a guide to Action', and a 'Commitment to Action by the Government'. At the beginning of the document there is a section entitled 'The Nature and Purpose of Planning' which might have been expected to clarify the objectives and make it clear what planing is about. After stating that in a mixed economy Government exerts influence through the public sector as well as taxation and this influence can be used in maintaining a satisfactory balance of payments, speeding up the working of the market economy, maintaining competition and providing social goods, the document goes on to extol the virtues of forecasting as a means of helping firms and industries to take more informed decisions and as a useful control device. However, as has been pointed out,[1] 'The Plan is not merely a projection, or even a forecast, for, while it rests partly on extrapolations of past trends, supplemented by forecasts of changes in these trends which there is reason to believe may come about before 1970, it also calls for expansion beyond these

[1] Geoffrey Denton, 'The National Plan—its contribution to Growth', *Planning* No. 493, November 1965.

indications.' Thus a simple projection would give a figure of 3 per cent per annum as the growth of exports by volume estimated on the basis of past performance. However, the Plan forecast a growth of 4 per cent per annum to 1970 by allowing for expected improvements in the prospects for exports, while the expansion required to achieve a surplus on the balance of payments planned for 1970 is, however, $5\frac{1}{4}$ per cent. While it is useful to have an evaluation of the changes expected as a result of Government policy, great care has to be taken to ensure that figures are quoted in the right context. The difference between projected, forecast and planned figures is highly important.

THE PREPARATION OF THE PLAN

The making of the National Plan involved a great number of people and organisations. It was essentially a political document and opened with a political statement, namely, 'the publication by the Government of a Plan covering all aspects of the country's economic development for the next five years is a major advance in economic policy-making in the United Kingdom. Prepared in the fullest consultation with industry, the Plan for the first time represents a statement of Government policy and a commitment to action by the Government.' The consultation of industry was carried on through the Economic Development Committees set up by the N.E.D. Office and various other representative bodies on both sides of industry. Co-ordination of this effort was secured through an inter-Departmental Working Party guided by a Steering Group under the Chairmanship of Sir Donald MacDougall, the Director General of the D.E.A. The members of the Working Party were drawn from the N.E.D. Office, the Bank of England, and the Government departments concerned with economic policy. Rather surprisingly for a body with such wide terms of reference, the Working Party in turn set up a number of sub-groups charged with the task of examining and reporting back on particular aspects of the Plan. The most notable of these dealt with the balance of payments, public expenditure, investment, manpower and so on. The political decisions on which the Plan was based such as the selection of a 25 per cent growth in national output from 1964 to 1970, decisions on the allocation of resources between investment, public expenditure, the removal of the deficit in the balance of payments, were fixed points all resulting from Ministerial decisions. The estimates contained in Part II of the National Plan—the Basis for Growth—were all prepared centrally. The N.E.D. Council was consulted on the choice of period for the Plan and on the target rate of growth. Once these had been agreed the basis on which the Plan would be prepared was virtually fixed.

Consultation with industry on these matters was intended to help in estimating the pattern of industrial growth, the probable demand for labour and new capital equipment and the measures necessary to attain a 25 per cent growth rate in the years to 1970. Consultation with industry was carried out in two separate stages. In the first industries were asked to provide estimates of their output, exports, employment and investment needs to 1970 on the basis of a 25 per cent growth rate. They were also asked to give their assessment of the conditions that would be needed if these estimates were to be realised. In the second stage meetings were held with representatives of the N.E.D. Office and Government departments at which the answers provided by industry were reviewed in comparison with aggregate estimates which had been made centrally in the departments.

The information which industries were asked to supply was set out in a questionnaire drafted by the inter-departmental Working Party.

Industries were asked to estimate demand for their products at home and abroad, and the proportion of the home market likely to be held by imports in 1970 on the assumption of a 25 per cent growth rate. They were also asked whether they would find it necessary to revise their present-day plans in order to meet these forecast needs. Similar questions were asked about investments and labour requirements to meet the 1970 output estimates, and firms' present expectations. On investment a distinction was drawn between definite commitments before a firm's money had been allocated and estimates of future spending on the basis of present plans and expectations. There were also questions about the consumption of the principal raw materials and fuels, particularly regarding imports of these, and whether any particular changes in the use of materials and fuels were expected. Firms were also asked to give separate estimates of qualified and skilled employees needed in 1970 and for information about trends in demand for particular types of skill and qualifications, and also to indicate the expected shortages. Where whole industries were involved, the questionnaire sought information regarding estimates, employment and investment between the different regions.

The questionnaire suffered from hasty preparation and the need to gather material quickly. If it had been part of an academic exercise carried out by a research institute, it would have come in for praise from the reviewers for the way it set out the information required from a hypothetical typical industry, and the way in which this could be adapted to the requirements of specific industries. In practice, however, it turned out to be a wasted opportunity producing information which was largely unrealistic because of the assumptions upon which it was based. The responsibility for the completion of the questionnaire rested with the Economic Development Committees. However, as there were only about a dozen of these in operation early enough to take part in the exercise, the greater part of the inquiry was carried out under special arrangements made by the N.E.D. Office or the sponsoring departments. Even where Economic Development Committees existed, the time allowed was not generally sufficient for the full committee to decide how it should be adapted to the particular needs of its industry, and the usual procedure was therefore for the N.E.D. Office to arrange a working party including representatives of the industry to carry out this task. After that the questionnaire was passed by the N.E.D. Office to trade associations or other representative bodies for the preparation of draft answers which were then considered by the Economic Development Committee.

The trade associations carried out inquiries amongst their own members in order to decide on the answers which should be given for the industry. They were expected to find out what knowledgeable people in the industry thought about their sales prospects at home and abroad in 1970, on the assumption of a 25 per cent national growth rate, and about their requirements for investment and labour. Information about the plans and expectations of individual firms were more difficult to obtain as these were necessarily confidential. The usual practice, where this was possible, was to carry out a confidential sample inquiry. There were, of course, frequent discussions between the trade association and the N.E.D. Office in the course of the industrial inquiry.

There were two industries where it was not possible to use trade associations to carry out the inquiry. In the distributive trades, where there is no single representative body, the estimates were prepared in the first place by a sub-committee of the Economic Development Committee whose members included representatives of a number of large firms and trade associations within the industry. There was a similar difficulty in mechanical engineering where there are a number of large firms but no single trade association to represent them. In this case the Board of Trade sent out a questionnaire on behalf of the Economic Development Committee to a sample of the largest firms, and it was on the basis of the replies to this that the results for the industry were prepared. The nationalised industries presented a much simpler problem as they were either single bodies or had central co-ordinating organisations.

Industries in the private sector which had no Economic Development Committee were dealt with either by N.E.D. Office or by their sponsoring departments. The usual practice was for the questionnaire to be sent to trade associations by the N.E.D. Office or the department concerned, after which the procedure was much the same as for industries with Economic Development Committees. The main difference was that in these cases trade unions were much less closely concerned than in industries where union members sat on the Economic Development Committee. Right at the end of the list there were a number of industries which were not concerned at all in the inquiry. These included a large group of miscellaneous service industries and other industries where it was not possible to find a representative organisation with a sufficiently wide coverage to enable the information to be obtained. In these cases the sponsoring departments made estimates on their behalf which were included in the inquiry. The Treasury and other departments concerned supplied estimates for the Health and Education services and the Public Administration, all of which use resources and contribute to the National Product.

The questionnaire went out at the end of January 1965 and replies were asked for by the beginning of April for the questions covering the 1970 estimates. Further details and comments on the estimates had to be sent in by a later date in April. Many industries experienced difficulty in providing estimates of the total of firms' expectations or intentions for output, investment, employment and exports in the years immediately ahead. In any case, firms have difficulty in summarising in a few figures what their plans and expectations will be in two or three years' time. It would make the life of forecasters very much easier if companies could say exactly what they would be doing in one, let alone five years' time. However, it is in the nature of business that what happens next year depends very much on what happens this. Tomorrow's expansion depends on today's sales and an inquiry which is based on the assumption that all expectations will be fulfilled is bound to be wildly optimistic. It must be remembered that the industrial inquiry depended on the willingness of top firms to supply information. It was not possible to make the inquiry in any way comprehensive and the results that came in were based on samples of varying validity. In short, when the sums were done the correctness of the answers depended not on the arithmetic but on how far the figures could be regarded as in any way representing the present and future situation in industry. In far too many cases what purported to be the plans and expectations of an industry were in fact the views of a relatively small sample of companies written up by the officials of the trade association and accepted by a more or less representative committee of the association. For many companies the concept of a 25 per cent growth rate had no very clear meaning in terms of their own activities. This is certainly the case in such industries as confectionery and clothing, in some parts of which it is extremely difficult to look ahead for a number of years.

The industrial inquiry as originally conceived had all the appearance of being a valuable part of the whole planning exercise. In fact it was its insistence on the need to prove the assumptions on which the Plan was based, notably the 25 per cent growth rate, that made it unworkable in practice. In theory industries and firms were given the opportunity of stating their actual investment plans as far ahead as they could, at the same time they were asked to look at these in terms of the 25 per cent growth assumption. This meant that the results of the inquiry were of doubtful value in estimating the development of the economy. Nor did it provide information which enabled a picture of existing strengths and weaknesses of British industry to be built up. Reading Part II of the National Plan, the so-called Industry Annexes, it is unusual to come across anything which throws light on the problems or prospects of the industries reported on. Not surprisingly the results of the industrial inquiry did not tally with the estimates obtained by using the Social Accounting Matrix Input/Output Model (SAM) which were published by the Cambridge Department of Applied Economics in *Exploring 1970*. Attempts were made to reconcile estimates made centrally with the results of the industrial inquiry at so-called 'dialogue' meetings which took place in May 1965 between representatives of industry and the N.E.D. Office and the sponsoring departments, as well as the Economic Development Committees. To some extent these meetings were concerned with discrepancies but also provided an opportunity for discussing the difficulties in preparing the answers to the questionnaire and for seeking explanations on how particular answers had been arrived at and what their significance could be taken to be. The 'dialogue' meetings had to be carried out against the pressure of time. There was the difficulty that changes in one industry's estimates resulting from one of these meetings would affect the demand of other industries. In no case, however, was it possible to have more than two 'dialogue' meetings for any industry. The meetings were valuable in producing a number of revisions of unrealistic estimates and in improving the consistency of the report as a whole. In some cases there were downward revisions of estimates and requirements and a number of changes both up and down in estimates of investment in 1970. The estimates of exports produced by the industrial inquiry were surprisingly optimistic. One reason for this was that firms replying to the questionnaire tended to be on the whole the best organised and the ones most likely to have a good export performance. In the case of mechanical engineering the inquiry was carried out by the Board of Trade on the basis of a sample inquiry among the larger firms to which less than half of those approached responded. In this case the final stage of carrying out the industrial inquiry came when the 'dialogue' meetings had been completed.

Annexes on the various industries were then prepared which were published in Part II of the National Plan. For the most part these were put together in the N.E.D. Office and other departments. The way in which the industrial inquiry was carried out did not impress industry. Criticisms were heard in the first months of 1965. Keith Richardson writing in the *Sunday Times* Business News asked if the exercise was totally valueless but decided that it was not if it was used as a basis for a factual N.E.D. Office report, saying, for example, 'that forecast demand for machine operators was far out of line with prospective supply'. This, however, was not what was to be done with the material collected. Instead, 'all these unreliable figures had to be fitted into each other and then made to produce a clearly internal consistency, and the result would be published as the National Plan'. This is in fact what happened. This same point was taken up in a lecture by Mr. Austin Albu, M.P., then Minister of State at the Department of Economic Affairs, at a luncheon given by the Market Research Society in London on Thursday, 27th May 1965.[1] He said: 'The inquiries being undertaken into industry are not just statistical exercises but are designed to spotlight difficulties and lead to action designed to treat them. The subsequent dialogues which are going on in the "Little Neddies" are throwing up a number of problems, the

[1] Reprinted in Eaton Paper No. 4, Institute of Economic Affairs..

solution of which enable us to achieve a substantially faster rate of economic growth.' In practice this confrontation did not lead to any new examinations of the problems. However, where it has taken place in the Economic Development Committees subsequently, it has in several cases led, as Mr. Albu suggested it would, to improved performance. The National Plan contains a deprecatory paragraph on the imperfections of its forecasts. This states that

some of the forecasts or projections for particular industries will inevitably turn out to be wrong. But this does not mean that it is useless to make them. Many progressive firms already look ahead in quantitative terms for up to five years and sometimes more. The projections in the Plan are essentially attempts by Government and industry, working in co-operation, to break down the general objectives of a 25 per cent growth rate into the implications for particular industries. These projections should help firms and industries to take more informed decisions than if they were left in the dark about other peoples' intentions and beliefs.[1]

Looking at the forecasts in retrospect it would be interesting to know how many companies felt that they were less in the dark as a result of reading the Industrial Annex covering their particular activities than they were before.

THE CONTENT OF THE PLAN

It is unlikely that anything quite like the National Plan will be published again in this country. It is therefore interesting to examine its contents and aspirations. It consisted of four parts:

1. The Planning Outline.
2. The Basis for Growth.
3. Industrial Section.
4. The use of Resources.

The first part sets out the 25 per cent growth target and explains that this has been chosen in the light of past trends in national output and output per head.

It involved achieving a 4 per cent annual growth rate well before 1970 and an average of 3·8 per cent between 1964 and

[1] The National Plan, Part I, para. 13.

1970. The achievement of this rate of increase in total output depended on a rate of progress of productivity and the rate of increase of the labour force. This last had been increasing by 0·6 per cent over the last decade and from 1965 on this rate of increase was likely to be very much less and on current trends would average 0·25 per cent per annum.

However, the greater part of the increase in output would have to come from an increase in productivity. After allowing for fluctuations in the rate of increase in productivity the Plan decided that the underlying growth of output per head would have to increase from nearly 2·75 per cent which it had been over the period of 1960 to 1964 to 3·4 per cent in the years to 1970. The measures that had been taken to redress the balance of payments would make the 25 per cent objective more difficult to achieve. But the Plan stated that it would still be possible provided productive capacity was extended despite the temporary check to the growth of demand, and provided management and workers maintained their efforts to improve efficiency in the use of both capital and labour and the competitiveness of British goods in foreign markets.

This part of the Plan also contained a check list of action required. This was set out under general headings covering Monetary Payments, Industrial Efficiency, Manpower Policy, Regional Policy, Public Spending, and Periodic Reviews. In each case the policy recommendation or attention required appeared on the left and the body responsible on the right. References to sections of the Plan in which the item was mentioned were given in each case. It was noted in the Plan:

The list shows many things that have to be done by Government, by the Economic Development Committees generally, by other bodies. It does not include many detailed things mentioned throughout the Plan that have to be done by particular industries; that would have made the list unmanageably long. But these detailed actions are essential to the fulfilment of the Plan. Of more fundamental importance is the action of individual managers and individual workers. Without their active co-operation, involvement and understanding, the Plan cannot succeed.

The second part of the Plan dealt with the basis of progress, covering output, productivity and the demand for labour, manpower, industrial efficiency, investment, prices and incomes, the balance of payments, and regional planning. This section contained forecasts of demand for various resources in 1970. It also described the work of the Economic Development Committees in the course of a discussion on ways and means of increasing industrial efficiency. In so far as the Plan can be regarded as a guide to future policy developments, this section was by far the most interesting. Chapter VIII on regional planning, for example was perhaps the most detailed statement on Government regional policy which had so far appeared.

Part III, dealing with the Industrial Sectors, linked the 25 per cent growth rate to the performance of individual industries and restated Government policy. Chapter XI, Energy, was of particular importance in restating Government policy with regard to the coal industry and its belief that the market would contract well below the 200 million tons a year which the National Coal Board had hoped to maintain. As the publication of the National Plan preceded the appearance of the White Paper on Fuel Policy,[1] the Energy chapter provided perhaps the best example of the way in which departments were brought to agree on the policy decisions of the Plan before its publication. Indeed, the National Plan marked the change-over from the policy of protecting coal as the major indigenous fuel to one of providing the cheapest energy possible in the interests of industry as a whole. This policy involves both economic and social problems as it is clearly not sound economics to burden the coal industry with the social costs of concentrating its production in profitable pits and closing the rest. A revised statement of the Government's objectives was given in the 1967 White Paper,[2] published in November 1967. There was some comment at the end of this section on the questions raised by the phasing of the growth of national output in the Plan. The most critical of these were stated to be the development of the balance of payments, the course of productive

[1] Fuel Policy, Cmnd. 2798, Ministry of Power, October 1965.

[2] Fuel Policy, Cmnd. 3438, Ministry of Power, November 1967.

investment in private industry and the speed with which productivity and productive capacity could be increased. According
to the Plan, the indications were that faster growth of output
would take place in the latter part of the period to 1970.
The allocation of resources in the first part of the period would
reflect the fact that the major part of improvement in the
balance of payments would have to be achieved in the first
years or so. This prediction was in the event proved to be
correct.

Part II of the Report consisted of the Industry Annexes.
These had been prepared in the N.E.D. Office and the
D.E.A. on the basis of the material supplied by industry.
Forty-three industries of one kind or another were covered in
this section. The most interesting part of each annex was the
concluding section on Conditions for Growth. This was the
place where the trade associations and other interests consulted
were able to get away from the questionnaire and mention some
of the things that were really bothering them. For example, the
motor car industry placed 'great emphasis . . . on government
action to remove trade barriers by removing the temporary
import surcharge . . . by reopening negotiations to join the
E.E.C. and by securing agreement in the Kennedy Round
negotiations for multilateral reductions of tariffs'. The Mechanical Engineering Annex stated that 'Certain companies feel
that Corporation Tax arrangements may lessen the encouragement given by investment allowances, and they are concerned
that the effectiveness of the latter should be maintained.' The
Annex on Newspapers and Periodicals drew attention to the
problems of overstaffing and demarcation in the national press
and also asked for 'further promotion of exports of periodicals'.
The furniture-makers pointed out that 'any measure having a
depressing effect on consumer demand will adversely affect
production' in the furniture industry. The Pottery Annex
agreed that improvement of productivity rested largely with
the industry and depended on the employment of more
scientists and technically qualified people, more investment and
further rationalisation of the production and structure of the
industry. However, it went on to point out that the Govern-

ment could help by 'assisting the industry to extend and invest in the Stoke on Trent region, where the technology of the industry is concentrated, to correcting tariff disparities where possible, to derating kilns, and reducing the cost of national insurance on part-time married women workers'. The construction industry, which had been under severe criticism, produced the longest section on conditions for growth of all the annexes. This repeated various suggestions that had been put forward by the industry and emphasised that these would be examined by the Economic Development Committees for the building industry and for the civil engineering industry. In particular, the report pointed out that the conditions in the industry were affected by the Government's deflationary measures of the 27th July 1965 which the Economic Development Committee had no opportunity of considering before the completion of the annex.

Finally, the Plan contained three appendices. The first dealt with regional differences in supply and demand for labour. The second contained regional studies on the West Midlands, North West, Scotland, Wales, the Northern Region, North East England and Northern Ireland. The third appendix was the questionnaire for the industrial inquiry.

VI
Regional Planning's New Look

1 OLD PROBLEMS—NEW ANSWERS

Seen from the centre the regional problem is basically one of a permanent imbalance in activity in the economy. The level of employment in the different regions of the country varies widely and as the N.E.D.C. report, *Conditions Favourable to Faster Growth*, pointed out, the object of policy is 'to prevent unemployment rising to politically intolerable levels and expenditure to this end is often considered a necessary burden to the nation, unrelated to any economic gain that might accrue from it'. The problem of the depressed areas had already received widespread public attention long before the Second World War. In 1934 an Act of Parliament officially recognised the existence of Special Areas where unemployment was particularly high and outside help was needed to secure economic development. There were four of these Special Areas, namely, the North East coast, West Cumberland, Central Scotland, and South Wales and Monmouthshire. Northern Ireland, where economic development was also backward, came under a separate set of regulations. The task of the Special Commissioners appointed under the 1934 Act was to attract light industry from the Midlands and South to the Special Areas. By 1938 some £21 million had been spent or allocated to the purchase of land, building of factories and the setting up of ten trading estates. In spite of all this activity, unemployment persisted at a high level.

While some areas were suffering from a surplus of labour and shortage of jobs, others were already displaying the symptoms of congestion. The over-population of London and the South Eastern area was studied by a Royal Commission under the chairmanship of Sir Montague Barlow which published its report in 1940. This recommended the setting up of a National Industrial Board to organise the dispersal of industry from the over-populated over-developed areas, to supervise the decentralisation and control the balance of industry. The Board was to have regional offices and the construction or extension of all industrial buildings would have been referred to it. The proposals put forward by the Barlow Commission were shelved on account of the war but some of them have been revived again in recent years.

In the last twenty years it has become clear that the principle of bringing work to the workers was not a complete answer to the imbalance in the structure of the British economy. The unemployment problem in the 1950s and 1960s was completely different from that of the inter-war period. Then the national average unemployment level was generally above 10 per cent and regional 'black spots' had unemployment rates of 20 per cent and upwards. Official policy therefore centred on attempts to combat general unemployment and dealt with structural problems as a secondary objective. Today the situation is relatively much more favourable with a national unemployment rate of around 2 per cent and levels of 4 per cent and over in the development districts. In periods when demand rises sharply the problem of general unemployment virtually disappears although expansion in the development districts will continue to be below the national average. These higher regional levels are extremely difficult to eradicate. However, the unemployed in the development districts are a valuable national resource which could make a substantial contribution to national employment and economic growth given the opportunity. The problem is complicated by the fact that the relatively high unemployment rates in the less prosperous regions are accompanied by low activity rates. The activity rate was defined by the N.E.D.C. as the proportion of civilian employees—employed plus registered unemployed—in a given

83

population age group.[1] Differences in regional activity rates are due to variations in the proportion of the population which can be regarded as potentially economically active. How many older men or married women would be able and willing to work if opportunities were available in the less prosperous regions, it is impossible to say. There is no doubt however that the effective size of the working population could be greatly increased if activity rates were as high in the less prosperous regions as they are in London and the South East and the Midlands.

A number of measures affecting regional development were passed in the years immediately after the war. The New Towns Act of 1946 was concerned with the redistribution of industry and the prevention of an unbalanced urban growth. Under this Act twenty-one new towns were authorised. Some of these were intended to absorb an excess of population from overcrowded centres such as London and Glasgow. Others were built as growth points to attract industry to particular areas where opportunities for industry activity were considered to be good. Examples of this type of development are Corby in Northamptonshire, Aycliffe and Peterlee in Co. Durham, Skelmersdale in Lancashire, Cwmbran in Monmouthshire and Livingstone in Scotland.

The building of each new town is under the supervision of a Development Corporation which has power to acquire sites by negotiation or if necessary by compulsory purchase. The Ministry of Housing and Local Government decides on the location of new towns, the funds needed being covered by a loan from the Treasury.

There are now twenty-two new towns in Britain and proposals have been announced for various others including Leyland/Chorley and Warrington/Risley in Lancashire, the Bletchley area in North Buckinghamshire and extensions of the existing towns of Ipswich, Northampton and Winchester. The last three are intended to provide jobs and homes for people moving out from the London area. Other new towns are projected in connection with plans for regional development

[1] *Conditions Favourable to Faster Growth*, para. 59.

on Humberside, on the Severn and in Mid-Wales and Eastern Scotland.

As new towns are finished the development corporation is dissolved and its assets and liabilities are handed over to a central agency, the Commission for the New Towns. This body which was created by the New Towns Act of 1959 supervises the final stages of the growth of new towns and their handing over to the control of a local authority. Crawley, Hemel Hempstead, Hatfield and Welwyn Garden City have all been handed over to the Commission.

New towns receive preferential treatment in the granting of industrial development certificates by the Board of Trade. This preference is now exercised more particularly in favour of new towns in development areas rather than those in the Midlands and South East. As well as encouraging manufacturing companies to establish themselves in the new towns, the Government is now urging firms in the service industries to move there.

The increase in the number of commercial and service businesses, company headquarters and the like set up in new towns serves to provide a wider range of employment for the growing numbers of school leavers. Encouragement to move out is given by the Location of Offices Bureau (L.O.B.), a commission appointed and financed by Government. The Bureau has three main functions: accumulating information; promoting publicity for moving from congested Central London; and providing information and advice. L.O.B. is able to supply information on the availability and cost of office accommodation and sites outside the London area, the staff position, transport and communications, educational facilities, the local housing situation and details of schools and othe amenities. Not surprisingly, taking a decision to move out of London is a slow process involving all kinds of considerations. An organisation such as L.O.B., while helping to persuade companies to move by providing them with all the available information, cannot take any positive steps to ease congestion. In spite of the inconveniences and frustrations of congestion, there are many who would still agree that this is no bad thing.

Another measure affecting the structure of industry was the

G

Distribution of Industry Act of 1954 which followed on the ideas put forward in the Act of 1934. A number of new 'development areas', as they were now called, were created, including Wrexham, South Lancashire, Merseyside, the Scottish Highlands, and North East Lancashire. The Commissioners of the 1934 Act were replaced by a Directorate responsible for the Location of Industry under the Board of Trade. This Directorate acquired sites and built factories for leasing to industry. The distribution of financial aid from the Treasury was extended by an Act of 1958 to include non-industrial activities and areas of high unemployment in addition to the development areas.

The third major innovation in policy to deal with the problem of regional imbalance was the Local Employment Act of 1960. This Act introduced the concept of small development districts instead of the large development areas. Whereas previously there had been eight development areas, under the new Act there were to be 165 development districts of limited size. A development district was defined as an area which according to Board of Trade statistics had a persistently high rate of unemployment. A high rate was taken to be 4·5 per cent or over, but this rate could be varied by the Board of Trade in agreement with the Ministry of Labour and Ministry of Transport. The list of development districts was also flexible and was in fact changed on several occasions by the Board of Trade in the light of developments in the employment position. Many of the development districts were within the former development areas but a number of entirely new ones had appeared, for example, in South West England. The method of assistance was similar to that used under the 1934 and 1945 Acts and consisted of the building of factories that were then leased, usually for a twenty-one-year period, at favourable rents, or sold on deferred terms. Capital grants were made available directly to the industrialist building a factory in the development district together with loans for acquiring working capital or equipment. Local authorities wishing to clear derelict sites could also obtain financial help from the Government. The Act also replaced the industrial estate companies set up under the Distribution of Industry Act by three industrial estate management corporations, one each for England, Wales and Scotland, financed by, and under the control of, the Board of Trade. The Local Employment Act gave the Board considerable powers to direct industry to particular parts of the country, through the granting or withholding of Industrial Development Certificates. These certificates had to be obtained for new buildings or extensions of 5,000 sq. ft. or more in area. The fact that office employment was not controlled by the Act was sharply criticised as leaving a wide range of development outside the Government's powers of direction.

REGIONAL POLICY SINCE 1964

The setting up of the Department of Economic Affairs following the General Election of October 1964 introduced a considerable change into the organisation and direction of regional economic policy. The new department took over as one of its functions the responsibility for regional policy and planning from the Board of Trade. One of the two Joint Parliamentary Secretaries of the D.E.A. was given the specific task of looking after regional affairs.

On 10th December 1964 the First Secretary of State for Economic Affairs, Mr. George Brown, announced a comprehensive Regional Planning system to maintain economic expansion through balanced regional growth. The new system was to be operated by entirely new administrative arrangements. England was divided into eight Planning Regions while Wales, Scotland and Northern Ireland were given their own planning machinery. The new regions in England were: Northern, Yorkshire and Humberside, North West, East Midlands, West Midlands, South West, East Anglia and the South East. In each Region there were to be two separate regional economic planning bodies—a Council and a Board. In Scotland and Wales a similar structure was created by the respective Secretaries of State who themselves became chairmen of their own Regional Economic Planning Councils.

Regional Economic Planning Councils consist of part-time voluntary members appointed by the Secretary of State for Economic Affairs. They are not delegates for particular interests but are chosen as individuals selected to be representative of widely differing types of experience, ideas and attitudes in their regions. The Regional Planning Boards consist of senior civil servants from the Government departments in the various regions, meeting with an Under-Secretary from the Department of Economic Affairs as Chairman. The Boards have their offices in what are regarded as the 'Regional capitals'. The terms of reference given to the Regional Economic Planning Councils are as follows:

1. To assist in the formulation of regional plans having regard to the best use of the Region's resources.

2. To advise on the steps necessary for implementing the Regional plans on the basis of information and assessments provided by the Regional Economic Planning Boards.

3. To advise on the regional implications of national economic policies.

The Boards have no specific terms of reference. According to the D.E.A. *Progress Report* of January 1965, their task is 'to prepare the Regional Plan, to co-ordinate the regional work of various Government departments concerned in its implementation'. The relationship of the new bodies to local authorities in the regions has never been closely defined. The *Progress Report* already quoted stated that 'they will work in close collaboration with [local authorities], and the Planning Councils will include members with local government experience'.

The new organisations were set up during 1965. The first Councils to appear were those for Scotland, Wales, the North, North West and West Midlands. These were followed by Yorkshire and Humberside, the East Midlands and the South West. In August 1965 the Government's decision on the planning machinery for South Eastern England was announced. This divided the area into two regions, East Anglia and the rest of the South East, with separate Councils and Boards for each. The members of the East Anglian Regional Economic Planning Council were named in December and those for the South East in February 1966.

The main event affecting the development of Regional

Economic Planning was the publication in September 1965 of the National Plan. This stated that:

Regional Planning is concerned with decisions to develop the infrastructure of the economy, and with the location of employment and population. Many of these decisions take a long time before they are fully effective. Thus the future of the Regions for many years ahead will be largely determined by many of the basic decisions about investment taken during the planned period, for example, in such things as new towns, major road and port schemes, these must be planned now for the 1970s, 1980s and 1990s, in line with the strategy for regional development.

Following the line taken in the N.E.D.C. report *Conditions Favourable to Faster Growth*, the National Plan stated that one of the major aims of regional policy must be to make use of the reserves of unused labour in regions where unemployment rates over the post-war period had been consistently high. It also pointed out that there might at times be some 'conflict' between the national priorities of economic growth and the local claims of certain regions or parts of them. However, the Plan went on to say that regional policies would not be concerned with 'bolstering up' small areas which have no economic future but with developing those parts of each region where there is a 'real growth potential'.

The Plan provided a number of new statistics for population density, employment and migration in the various Regions and surveyed the potentialities of each. It then set out measures which the Government could take to influence regional development. These were stated to lie in three main fields:

1. Public Investment programmes to modernise the infrastructure of the less prosperous and old industrial regions and reduce the congestion of the large cities. Here the Government would seek the help from the Regional Councils in taking regional needs into consideration when drawing up future investment programmes.

2. Measures to influence population distribution by catering in the short term in all regions for the movement of population (in particular to house urban overspill), and in the long term by pro-

viding for population growth in ways most conducive to national economic growth and the provision of a pleasant human environment.

3. Government action to stimulate regional growth in the less prosperous regions by influencing the geographical pattern of employment and economic activity. In this connection steps which the Government had already taken included the control of office development in the London Metropolitan region announced in November 1964, and later extended to the Birmingham connurbation, and the control over industrial location exercised by the issue of Industrial Development Certificates.

II LOCATION OF INDUSTRY

Responsibility for the location of industry rests with the Board of Trade. In August 1966 large parts of Britain were designated as Development Areas in which industry was to be encouraged to set up new factories. The new areas have replaced the previous smaller Development Districts and between them they cover Northern England, Merseyside, nearly the whole of Scotland, Wales, Cornwall and North Devon. All told they contain a fifth of Britain's working population. These areas have a higher than average level of unemployment and labour is likely to continue to be available for a number of years because of the presence in them of a number of declining industries. The decision to take larger areas was taken as a means of increasing the possibility of offering a wider choice of sites to incoming firms. This would increase the likelihood of attracting a larger number and greater variety of firms, and assist the policy of developing natural growth points within the region. The concept of growth points was one of the proposals put forward in the N.E.D.C. report *Conditions Favourable to Faster Growth*.

The Government offers a variety of inducements to new and expanding businesses in the Development Areas. Under the old system companies received initial and investment allowances as an inducement to set up new plants in the poorer areas. Under the Industrial Development Act 1966 these were replaced by cash grants. The new grants are given irrespective of a firm's profit or tax position so that it is possible to calculate their effect when investment decisions are being made. The processes which are eligible for cash grants include, broadly speaking, the manufacture of any article; extraction of minerals; construction and civil engineering; or scientific research related to any of these processes. Grants are not payable on road vehicles nor on such items as office machinery and furniture and canteen equipment. No distinction is made between British and imported plant and machinery, and grants are payable on the instalments of qualifying assets which are taken on hire purchase. Where assets are let on hire they are eligible for grants on certain conditions. Individual items costing less than £25 are not eligible for cash grant in any circumstances. The Development Areas benefit particularly from the new system of investment grants because whereas the general long-term rate of grant is 20 per cent of the capital cost of eligible plant and machinery, in Development Areas the long-term rate is 40 per cent. For the period between 1st January 1967 and 31st December 1968 the rates have been raised to 25 and 45 per cent respectively. Apart from plant and machinery which qualifies for investment grants because it is used in one of the patent processes used, computers, ships and hovercraft which are acquired for carrying out business in Britain are also eligible. The rate in this case is 20 per cent.

The Board of Trade can also provide help for projects which will increase employment in the Development Areas under the Local Employment Acts, 1960 to 1966. Under these Acts the Board may:

(a) Provide premises for rent or purchase;

(b) Pay grants of up to 25 per cent of the cost of erecting a new building or extending or adapting an existing one;

(c) Make loans for general purposes of undertaking in a Development Area whether new to the Area or an expansion of an existing business; and

(d) Pay grants towards unusual initial expenditure incurred in setting up business in a developing area or transferring an undertaking to one.

The buildings provided by the Board of Trade can be of standard type or designed to suit the applicant's particular requirements. Factories may also be built to rent or for sale, but very large or specialised factories that would be difficult to re-let if vacated are built for sale only. On the Industrial Estates, as distinct from individual sites, factories are usually rented. Leases for rented factories are normally for twenty-odd years at a rent assessed by the District Valuer on the basis of values current for the same sort of property in the district. Firms renting any Board of Trade factory for a new project may qualify for an initial rent-free period of two years in cases where special problems have been involved because of the distance from the firm's existing undertaking.

Other concessions to firms deciding to set up a factory in a Development Area include building grants and loans and grants for general expenditure. Building grants are payable to companies which purchase a new building or themselves build a new factory or extension or adapt existing premises. The rate of grant is 25 per cent of building costs including the purchase price of the site, site preparation, the cost of building, the provision of services and permanent fixtures. Where there are special problems a higher rate of 35 per cent may be paid at the Board's discretion. The deciding factor is the amount of the grant in relation to the employment to be provided. The Board consults the Board of Trade Advisory Committee (B.O.T.A.C.), an independent body of professional and businessmen, before reaching a decision on whether a particular project qualifies for a grant.

Loans and grants for general expenditure can be made for the purchase of buildings, plant, machinery and equipment (excluding the amount of any investment grant made), and for working capital. Repayment of a loan may be spread over a reasonable period and interest is fixed at a moderate rate. Grants, apart from investment and building grants, are offered only where an undertaking will incur initial expenses which are regarded as unusual either in nature or amount because of a project being located in a Development Area. The Board of Trade is only able to act on the advice of the Board of Trade Advisory Committee (B.O.T.A.C.). Companies have to provide information under a number of heads when asking for assistance. In particular they must give up-to-date accounts, not more than four months old, and furnish forward estimates in the form of Profit and Loss Accounts for a period of at least three years. In the case of loan assistance, companies are expected to provide a reasonable proportion of the necessary finance themselves and thus take a proper share of the risk.

The Ministry of Employment and Productivity also provides help for companies moving to the Development Areas as financial assistance under the Employment and Training Act 1948 towards the cost of training the additional labour required by firms starting or expanding undertakings in Development Areas. If a company sets up a temporary training school or training section, in rented accommodation in a Development Area, before its factory is built there, a special grant can be paid for a maximum period of two years. The Ministry also provides free training in skilled trades for employees in Government Training Centres, and for semi-skilled engineering occupations by the loan of instructors on assembly lines, processing packaging, bottling and so on, by special Training Within Industry (T.W.I.) courses. Full particulars of the services provided by the Ministry in the Development Areas can be had from the local office of the Ministry in the Area concerned.

In any move to a new area housing is one of the most important considerations. The Ministry of Housing and Local Government, the Scottish Development Council in Scotland, and the Welsh Office in Wales can help in providing houses for key workers in the new locality. Advice on this service can be provided by the Regional Offices of the Board of Trade.

Proposals for building new factories or extending old ones outside the Development Areas are strictly controlled. Before any proposal for building containing over 5,000 sq. ft. of new industrial space can be considered by a local planning authority in Britain, an Industrial Development Certificate must be granted by the Board of Trade. This control is operated stringently in the Midlands, London and the South East where the lower limit is 3,000 sq. ft. and the Board of Trade will issue certificates only if projects cannot be sited efficiently in regions with more free manpower. The Board also controls office development over 3,000 sq. ft. in the Midlands and the South East

93

TABLE

Investment Incentives—Old and New

	Grants	Tax allowances Investment	Initial
Existing System			
National			
New plant and machinery	—	30%	10%
Second-hand plant and machinery	—	—	30%
New industrial buildings and structures	—	15%	5%
Development Districts			
Plant and machinery for industrial undertakings:			
New	10%[1]	30%	Free depreciation
Second-hand	10%[1]	—	30%
Other plant and machinery:			
New	—	30%	10%
Second-hand	—	—	30%
New buildings and structures:			
Industrial	25%[1]	15%	5%
Non-industrial	25%[1]	—	—
New System			
National			
Plant and machinery:			
Qualifying for investment grants	20%	—	—
Not qualifying (includes second-hand)	—	—	30%
New industrial buildings and structures	—	—	15%
Development Areas			
Plant and machinery:			
Qualifying for investment grants	40%	—	—
Not qualifying (includes second-hand)	—	—	30%
New buildings and structures	25%[1] or 35%[2]	—	15%
Non-industrial	25%[1] or 35%[2]	—	—

[1] These grants are conditioned on an adequate provision of employment.

[2] The higher rate will only be given where the Board of Trade consider that the problems involved justify additional assistance.

and most applications are refused. This means that for the foreseeable future, Industrial Development Certificates are likely to be issued only in special circumstances for projects outside the Development Areas.

III PROSPECTS AND PROBLEMS

The Economic Planning Councils have been concerned with carrying out surveys of their areas which have been published as studies. The first of these to appear were from the North West and the West Midlands. The studies were not regarded as statements of policy but examinations of problems and possibilities. Both these regions were able to draw upon regional studies started under the previous Government. In the same fashion the Northern Region had at its disposal a plan of action for the North East laid down under Lord Hailsham. Other regions, however, had to start from the beginning. This was particularly the case in those areas where regional boundaries differed from those used by other Government departments.

The shelving of the National Plan following the announcement of the Government's emergency deflationary measures of 20th July 1966 did not greatly affect the objectives of the Regional Economic Councils and Boards. Their problem was still to find ways and means of implementing recommendations and proposals put forward in the studies which they had produced. The fact that the new regional organisations have no independent budgets places them in a position of influence without power. In those regions where most progress has been made in preparing studies and drawing up priorities for future development, the sense of frustration at not being able to proceed further, let alone faster, is greatest. Not surprisingly demand has arisen for an elected regional tier in the Government machine. At present, it is argued, the Regional Councils are operating without direct contact with the electorate. Their connection with local authorities in their region is tenuous and depends on the individual membership of the Council. However, when it comes to devising constituencies for such a body, considerable difficulties arise. Elections for County Borough, Borough and Urban District Councils, where interest

95

might be expected to be high, produce depressingly low polls. If the experience of County Councils is anything to go by, the chance to vote for members of an even more remote Regional Council would hardly set the populace alight. It may very well be that an appointed Council is better fitted to carry out the difficult task of assessing regional needs. In any case the sort of people who have the qualifications necessary for this kind of work are not always to be found among the active members of the political parties.

The new Regional Economic Planning arrangements have no formal powers. The Councils are exclusively advisory bodies and the Boards are inter-departmental committees of civil servants with no more authority than that possessed by their individual members. The preparation of the initial surveys of the problems of each region provided an immediate task for the Councils which, as the published studies show, was in most cases very effectively carried out. The question arises how long busy, highly qualified people will continue to devote their time and energies to the work of a system which has been described as 'planning by faith'. Against this view it is claimed that what really matters is that the Councils should give good advice and that this should be taken and acted upon by Government and local authorities. For certain types of problems requiring joint action by a number of different Government departments, this assertion is probably true within severe limitations.

The degree of success achieved by the Councils and Boards depends entirely on the personality and ability of their chairmen. These have the very daunting task of acting as innovators and at the same time not upsetting too many people already working in the same field. The division of power in decision-making between the Government and the regions is highly important. Broad decisions about the future capacity of each region to take the United Kingdom's increasing population can be taken at the centre but regional voices should decide how the expansion will be distributed through the regions. On the financial side there will need to be a recasting of existing financial procedures if regional councils are to exercise any control over the development within their boundaries. It may be that in future the national budget will first of all have to be divided regionally and then divided again departmentally for each region. This would demand a revolutionary change in long-established practices and it is very hard to see the Treasury or Government departments giving up authority in this way. For regional economic planning to be a success a new form of organisation involving decision-making and finance has to be evolved. This is not a party political matter but a question of changing attitudes which on the one hand are too parochial and on the other too ambivalent. It is the failure to take long-term decisions at the centre which is the real crux of the matter. Local authorities may be parochial in their attitudes but they can act within the context of the region in which they are situated. The region can only be an active unit if, in turn, it is given a realistic role to play as a part of the nation as a whole.

One other aspect of regional planning requires comment. In September 1967 manufacturers in Development Areas became eligible for a Regional Employment Premium (R.E.P.) on all workers for whom they could claim an S.E.T. premium. R.E.P. was intended to cure the regional imbalance by an extension of the S.E.T. principle. In other words it made manufacturing employment especially cheap in the Development Areas. In November 1967 following the devaluation of Sterling, S.E.T. premiums to manufacturers in the rest of the country were suspended. As a result, outside the Development Areas, manufacturers now paid S.E.T. and received their contributions back without premium after three months. Whether this arrangement improved employment prospects in the Development Areas is not known. It certainly made a deep impression elsewhere.[1]

[1] See for example *The Director*, May 1968, pp. 187–9.

VII

Changing the Structure of the Economy

The need to set aside the growth targets of the National Plan as a result of the deflationary measures taken on the 20th July 1966 led to a re-examination of the objectives of planning. In both the N.E.D.C. growth programme of 1963 and the National Plan the numerical projections looking four or five years ahead had been the most vulnerable parts of the operation. The new approach was described in the D.E.A. *Progress Report* for April 1967 which stated that 'much of the action needed to secure faster economic growth does not depend on detailed numerical projects (that is, projections of possible economic change in terms of figures and rates) but follows from the agreed need to improve our industrial efficiency and our balance of payments'. In other words, the emphasis was moving away from forecasting to the examination of ways and means of making the economy more efficient. The need for modernisation of the British economy had been one of the principal issues raised by the political parties in the General Election campaigns of October 1964 and March 1966. This emphasis represented a return to problems which had been discussed by the National Economic Development Council in its early days and which led to the publication of *Conditions Favourable to Faster Growth* in April 1963. Since that time the position had been considerably clarified without necessarily being improved. A number of new organisations had been set up and innumerable committees of inquiry had examined specific problem areas. The N.E.D.C. report had examined eight different problems.[1] From these it is

[1] See page 34 above.

possible to pick out three major themes on which action had been taken. These are regional policy, industrial training policy, and scientific and technical advance.

The N.E.D.C. report emphasised the fact that increases in productivity necessary for faster economic growth called for highly skilled management throughout the economy, not only in industry but in every type of organisation. While not entering into the controversial question of whether managers were born or made, the report stated bluntly that the qualities needed for management 'can be developed by the right kind of practical theoretical training while the actual techniques of most management jobs can be taught'. Management education involves providing for the needs both of young men entering industry and those already in executive positions, who are out of touch with more recently developed techniques. The provision of management training courses was, and indeed still is, divided between a variety of bodies. These include the education departments of local authorities, the universities, the specialised management bodies, management consultants, independent colleges, and organisations set up by industries and large companies. These various activities are to some extent co-ordinated by the United Kingdom Advisory Council on Education for Management consisting of representatives from both educational and industrial organisations.

As the universities have, hitherto, for the most part played only a minor role in management education, the main part of the work had been developed chiefly in the technical colleges and Colleges of Advanced Technology. The N.E.D.C. recommended that in addition to existing arrangements there was need 'for at least one very high level new school or institute somewhat on the lines of the Harvard Business School or the School of Industrial Management at the Massachusetts Institute of Technology, either as an independent institution or as part of some existing university or College of Advanced Technology'. This proposal was backed up strongly by the Robbins Committee on Higher Education, and the setting up of the London and Manchester Business Schools followed. Another development has been the granting of university status to

Colleges of Advanced Technology in April 1965. In bringing about improved industrial efficiency the quality of industrial management is of the first importance. The new Graduate Business Schools, together with the facilities for higher management education at the Colleges of Advanced Technology, the universities and other institutions are now able to meet a large part of the needs for training of this kind. Their efforts are supplemented by training provided for short- and medium-length courses by the Administrative Staff College at Henley, Ashridge College of Management, and the work of independent organisations able to call on the skills and experiences of leading industrialists as well as specialists in management education subjects and techniques.

The training of industrial managers is however only one side of the problem of modernisation so far as manpower is concerned. During the 1950s and early 1960s there was growing dissatisfaction with the state of industrial training in Britain. Recognised training methods were for the most part 'on the job', which meant that the apprentice or new entrant was attached to a qualified workman who taught him as much as he thought was good for him. The provision of industrial training was the business of each employer and while some firms developed highly efficient training schemes suitable to their needs, others were content to keep their training efforts to a minimum and recruit people outside whenever exceptional need arose. In industry as a whole insufficient people were receiving training of an adequate standard and many firms were not making a reasonable contribution towards the cost of training their workpeople. In March 1964 the Conservative Government passed the Industrial Training Act aimed at remedying these defects and securing an improvement in training at all levels from operative to manager, and at all ages from school leaver to adult, throughout industry and commerce. The Act followed on the White Paper on Industrial Training (Cmnd. 1892) of December 1962. Under the new Act industrial training became obligatory. A company now had the choice of training its own personnel or contributing to a pool established for its industry to cover the cost of setting up and operating training establishments. The Minister of Labour was empowered to establish Industrial Training Boards whose main responsibility is to ensure that training in their particular industries is adequate in quality and quantity. The cost of the Boards is covered by a levy which all employers under a particular Board are required to pay at a rate decided by the Board. Employers are entitled to receive a grant to cover the cost of training organised by themselves which is in accordance with the recommendations of the Board.

In May 1964 the Minister of Labour established a Central Training Council to advise him on 'the exercise of his function under this Act and on any other matter relating to the professional training which he may refer to it'. The Council has set up five committees dealing with General Policy, Commercial and Clerical Training, Research, Training of Training Officers, and Management Training and Development. There are also special committees for Scotland and Wales. At the end of 1965 ten Industrial Training Boards had been set up covering some seven million workers, that is, about one-third of industry. The first Boards established were for engineering, construction, iron and steel, and wool, all of which came into being in the summer of 1964. These were followed by shipbuilding in November 1964 and electricity supply, gas, water supply, and ceramics, glass and mineral products in the summer of 1965. In December 1965 the furniture and timber industries set up Industrial Training Boards. All Boards consist of a Chairman, an equal number of employer and worker members and a number of educational members.

A Board's first duty is to ensure that adequate training is provided in the industry for which it is responsible. To do this effectively it has to find out what training is being done, estimate future manpower requirements, both in quantity and type of skill and then take action to ensure that the training provided reaches these requirements. In the years since the Second World War there have been acute shortages of skilled manpower in certain industries and a number of the Boards have particular problems in this field. A Board can provide its own training courses or arrange for other organisations to do this.

H

There is nothing in the Industrial Training Act which compels firms to provide training for their employees. If they do not, however, they are still required to pay the levy fixed by the Board without receiving any grant in return. It is possible for firms providing substantial schemes to receive back in grants more than they have actually paid in levy.

The Industrial Training Boards are also required to publish recommendations about the nature, length, and content of training necessary to meet the requirements of their industries. These recommendations also cover methods of training and give guidance to companies wishing to establish or improve their own training arrangements. The Boards are also concerned with the provision of further education by day release to local technical colleges and other institutions. If workers are to be able to adapt themselves to technological change in the future, it is really necessary that they should have an educational background which includes technical and general education as well as practical training.

The amounts raised in levies by Industrial Training Boards are in some cases very considerable. The Training Board for the Engineering industry for example raised a levy which yielded £75 million in the first year. The efficiency of industrial training depends very largely on the quality of the instructors and training officers. There is a considerable shortage of suitable staff for this purpose and the Ministry of Labour have started a number of short courses to provide training for 1,100 instructors each year. There is no doubt that this is the principal weakness of the scheme and steps will have to be taken to increase the number and quality of staff available to man it. Some technical colleges are putting on courses for training officers but the numbers involved are by no means sufficient to meet the demand. One difficulty is that firms do not want to lose the services of good men released by them for courses as training officers, supervisors and instructors. It is not surprising therefore that the response from industry to appeals to support short courses of this kind has been disappointing.

Improved training arrangements are not by themselves enough to secure the better use of manpower needed for faster economic growth. Ways and means have to be found of over-coming obstacles to give adequate mobility of labour. These obstacles are a mixture of economic and social factors of which much the most important is the problem of housing. A variety of measures have been introduced in recent years to induce employees to establish factories in the development areas (see Chapter VI). Many of these are related to the provision of training arrangements through the Government Training Centres. Over thirty of these are now in operation with nearly 7,000 training places. Here also, however, it has proved ex-tremely difficult to find instructors in some trades and in some areas. Several of the Economic Development Committees have studied the training problems of their industries and the ways and means by which these can be improved. From these and the reports of the Industrial Training Boards the amount of information available for the future on training requirements will be considerably increased. While this is certainly a step in the right direction it remains to be seen whether the present arrangements can be sufficiently closely co-ordinated to provide an effective manpower and training policy.

THE INDUSTRIAL REORGANISATION CORPORATION

The National Plan emphasised the need for more concentration and rationalisation in industry as a means of promoting greater efficiency and international competitiveness. In January 1966, Mr. George Brown, then Secretary of State for Economic Affairs, issued a White Paper (Cmnd. 2889) containing pro-posals for the setting up of an Industrial Reorganisation Corporation with the task of speeding up re-groupings and mergers aimed at producing bigger and more efficient industrial units. The Corporation was to be empowered to acquire a stake in the ownership of new groupings or enterprises that it helped to create. However, it was not intended to be a general holding company on the lines of the Italian I.R.I. According to the White Paper the faster it turned over its capital the greater would be its capacity to promote the objects for which it was set up. The Corporation was given 'the right to draw as it needed' on £150 million from the Exchequer.

The coming of the 1966 General Election held up the passing of the legislation needed to implement the White Paper. The Corporation was nevertheless able to begin preliminary work under its Chairman Sir Frank Kearton (Chairman of Courtaulds) and its Managing Director Mr. Ronald Grierson, seconded from S. G. Warburg, the merchant bank.

The objections to selective intervention in the running of industry centre round the desirability of maintaining a framework of rules which apply equally to all men or all companies. Once Government, whether in the form of a special agency or under some other guise, begins to hand out rewards and punishments on the basis of decisions by particular officials, trouble is inevitable. Businessmen would be the first to admit that they are not all perfect and that they do not take advantage of all the opportunities for profitable investment that come their way. However, with so many private firms and merchant banks operating in the field of mergers and amalgamations it is hard to believe that there are many specific opportunities known to the officials of an *ad hoc* body such as the I.R.C., which have not been considered by industry.

Under Mr. Grierson's direction[1] the I.R.C. operated through a small staff able to move through industry gaining confidence and picking up ideas. Persuasion rather than directives were regarded as the most effective means of introducing changes. In contrast to this so-called 'soft' approach there is the 'hard' school argument, put forward by some Ministers, that if the I.R.C. is in business to change the structure of industry then it should get on with it and not be too squeamish about hurting people's feelings.

On the whole I.R.C. has followed an independent line and not acted on projects that the Government was anxious to push. The taking up of an I.R.C. shareholding in the Chrysler-Rootes merger was an exception to this general rule. In the G.E.C./A.E.I. merger the I.R.C. put forward a proposal for a merger between these two giant electrical engineering companies. This was turned down by A.E.I. but G.E.C. decided to go ahead with I.R.C. support and the merger eventually took

[1] He resigned in October 1967.

place. One problem in a case of this kind is the division of responsibility between Government departments. The D.E.A. has set up the I.R.C. to introduce changes in the structure of industry in the interests of efficiency which in many cases means producing bigger units. When this involves companies as big as G.E.C. and A.E.I. the question of monopoly positions arises. In such cases the arbiter of the public interest is the Board of Trade. If the Board decide that a particular case requires investigation then it refers it to the Monopolies Commission. If in any particular case the Commission decided that a merger in which I.R.C. was involved was creating a monopoly it would rule accordingly and presumably set out conditions under which, in its view, the merger could take place. This did not actually happen in the G.E.C./A.E.I. case but it is clear that the operations of the I.R.C. can produce considerable complications in a contested take-over. The fact that I.R.C. is in favour of the resulting merger can greatly strengthen the hand of the company making the bid. If an organisation is set up to do a particular job, as I.R.C. was, it is only to be expected that it will attempt to do it. The important point is that its existence puts companies in a position where they may have to justify their policies and actions to the extent of proving that their continued, independent existence is justified. This is a big step forward from the idea of hatching up general proposals for the better organisation of particular industries. It gives a new and potentially dangerous edge to Government intervention in the running of the economy.

SCIENTIFIC AND TECHNICAL ADVANCE

There has been in recent years a growing realisation that where the British economy has fallen badly behind is in productivity and investment. In the United States output per man is higher as a result of having two or three times as much horsepower per head installed in its factories as in Britain. For Britain to improve her performance scientific methods will have to be applied systematically to industry. This is not just a matter of providing training facilities for an increasing number of scientists and technologists but of ensuring that steps are taken to see that the existing stock of available qualified scientists and engineers is properly used. Both the Conservative and Labour parties have shown their awareness in different ways of the need for the State to take initiatives for securing faster scientific and technical advance. Expenditure on research and development in Britain is largely financed by the State and depends on Government decisions. In 1962 Britain spent 2·2 per cent of her Gross National Product on R and D compared with the 1·5 per cent for France and 1·3 per cent for West Germany. This figure has now risen to 2·6 per cent of G.N.P., which is below the 3·7 per cent of the United States, but still higher than any of the Continental countries. The total amount spent is not by itself decisive however. What matters is its distribution and the extent to which the 'fall out' from Government expenditure on Research and Development helps to modernise industry. There has been considerable criticism of the fact that a very large proportion of the Government R and D spending in recent years has gone to the aviation industry rather than to machine tools or computers. This is partly due to the fact that Britain's high spending on R and D is a factor of high defence expenditure. According to Professor P. M. S. Blackett[1] the R and D carried out in Britain is probably less than 10 per cent of the total carried out in the whole world. Much of the resulting know-how is transferred to other countries by licence agreements, through international companies or by straightforward copying. At its present level of expenditure Britain certainly cannot remain self-sufficient in technology. This means that a great deal of the production equipment installed in British factories and plants will be of foreign manufacture. One of the problems of recent years has been that an increasing proportion of all equipment which can increase productivity, especially of export goods, has been of this kind. If productivity is to be increased the growth of demand for the import of sophisticated foreign machinery and equipment must inevitably increase with consequent mounting strain on the balance of payments.

[1] Technology, Industry and Economic Growth, 13th Fawley Foundation Lecture, reproduced in *Esso Magazine*, Spring 1967.

The setting up of the Ministry of Technology alongside the Ministry of Education and Science was an indication of the importance attached by the Labour Government to scientific and technical advance. The various parts of the machinery through which the Government hopes to secure industrial modernisation can be summarised as follows. The Ministry of Education and Science, which combined the Ministry of Education and the Ministry of Science which had been created by the Conservative Government in 1959, has two main sections. The first of these is for education up to and including the secondary stage, and the other for higher education and scientific matters. The Ministry of Technology is the sponsoring Ministry for the aircraft industry, electronics and computers, machine tools, electrical and mechanical engineering and a number of other industries. It is also responsible for the Atomic Energy Commission and the National Research Development Corporation. The Department of Scientific and Industrial Research which had been responsible for the promotion of scientific research in its application in industry since 1916 was abolished by the Science and Technology Act of 1965 which followed on the report of the Trend Committee. Two new Research Councils, the Science Research Council and the Natural Environment Research Council, have been set up in its place. The former has taken over the University grant-awarding functions of the old D.S.I.R. and responsibility for basic scientific research. The Natural Environment Research Council deals with problems which are broadly 'ecological' in character. Some of the other research functions of the D.S.I.R. passed to the Ministry of Technology.

At the Ministry of Education and Science there is a Council for Scientific Policy which was set up with advisory powers in 1965. There is also a Committee on Manpower Resources for Science and Technology which advises the Ministry of Education and Science and the Ministry of Technology. In the latter Ministry there is also the Advisory Council on Technology. In addition, there is a Central Advisory Committee on Science of which the Government's Chief Scientific Adviser is Chairman.

Through these various channels the Government is spending

over £500 million a year on research and development. Of this the Secretary of State for Education and Science is responsible for about 40 per cent of Government spending on civil research, the Minister of Technology for 54 per cent, including aviation, while other departments between them spend the remaining 6 per cent. The Ministry of Technology is responsible for the research which is carried out by private enterprise on 'Development Contracts' through the National Research Development Corporation. Four industries, in particular, are operating in this way, namely, machine tools, electronics, computers and telecommunications, in all of which a high level of R and D spending is essential. The N.R.D.C. is also operating 'preproduction contracts' under which the Government provides an outlet for new products in the advanced machine tool industry. The N.R.D.C. is operating a £1 million scheme to enable producers of numerically controlled machine tools to offer these 'trial period terms' to prospective buyers. A National Computer Centre has been opened in Manchester, and contracts worth some £10 million from the universities for British-made computers and another £5 million from industry have been secured. The Ministry of Technology is also interested in improving the design of engineering products and has introduced various recommendations following the report of the Fielden Committee of 1963. These include the setting up of the Institute of Advanced Machine Tool and Control Technology.

The application of technology depends to a very large extent on the supply of qualified scientists and engineers. Many of the weaknesses of British industry and its failure to meet foreign competition can be attributed to a shortage of engineers and failure to make proper use of those available. Various measures have been taken to raise the status of engineers by the Ministry of Technology in conjunction with the Confederation of British Industry. The setting up of the Engineering Institutions Joint Council is a move by the engineering profession to raise standards and to co-ordinate training and conditions of entry to the professions. Professor Blackett has stated that there are probably too many qualified scientists and engineers in Britain working on research and too few on the later stages of design, production and sales. 'It is important not to duplicate research, and having a few large firms in a particular industry places us in a better position to fight overseas competition.'[1] The waste arising from the duplication of effort due to fragmentation is another important reason why Britain does not obtain full value from the qualified scientists and engineers now working in industry. In Britain 'with 16 million wired homes' there are 170 suppliers of electric fires turning out over 1,000 different models, i.e. seven models for each maker, with each model showing an average annual sale of only £1,200.'[2] The same sort of duplication and effort is to be found in the manufacture of other consumer durable goods. Even more serious is the fact that in the production of capital goods there are no less than sixteen firms in Britain making high-power electrical transformers, while in West Germany there are only six.

Although Britain's effort in the field of technology is open to criticism, it is nevertheless considerable compared with that of the continental European countries. The position broadly is that Western Europe as a whole (E.E.C. and E.F.T.A.) spend about one-quarter as much as the United States on R and D. If allowance is made for the fact that costs, especially salaries, are about twice as high in the United States, then the Western European effort looks a little more respectable. But even if it is assumed that American R and D expenditure is only double that of Western Europe, the position is still unsatisfactory. The British contribution to the West European total, which in terms of money is of the order of £1,000 million a year in R and D spending for the public and private sectors, represents two-thirds of the total amount spent by the continental countries. Britain is fortunate in having managed to keep abreast of new developments in for example nuclear physics and aero engines, and to have maintained a computer industry. There have been a number of important technical developments in British industry that have resulted in new industrial applications such as the Pilkington Float Glass process. The fact remains, however, that the money spent on research in Britain has in all too

[1] 13th Fawley Foundation Lecture.
[2] Nicholas A. H. Stacey, *Mergers in Modern Business*, Hutchinson 1967.

many cases produced ideas which have not been developed here because of the heavy expense involved.

It is frequently argued that one of the great advantages of joining the E.E.C. would be that it would give British industry access to a market big enough to support a greatly increased level of R and D expenditure. If this is the case, it would be expected that German and French companies operating in a market of 180 million people would by now enjoy some of these advantages. In fact experience in the E.E.C. has been disappointing in this respect. The Common Market is still a very different proposition from the American market with its continent-wide system of commercial laws and procedures. The Six are held back by restrictive regulations on amalgamations and mergers, by differences in their educational systems and academic qualifications, and by the fact that national company laws have prevented the setting up of 'European' companies.

This lack of technological progress in industry in Britain and the E.E.C. has been marked by an increasing dependence on the United States for systems and technical processes. On purely financial grounds it is clearly impossible, even if it were desirable, for Britain to try to match the American defence programme in the hope that the 'spin-off' from this will raise the level of industrial achievement. At the same time, the measures now being taken to re-organise Government spending on defence, education and scientific research will have to be better co-ordinated if we are to secure higher value in terms of R and D achievement for the money spent. To a great extent this is a matter of deciding on priorities. Just as decisions have to be taken about Britain's political role in the world, equally important decisions must be made about what we are trying to do in the field of technology. There seems little point in trying to duplicate what the Americans and Russians are doing in their space programmes. The number of people likely to be upset because the first man on the moon comes from Phoenix or from Minsk rather than from Liverpool cannot be great. It has been suggested[1] that we should concentrate our effort on

[1] A. C. Copisarow in a paper at the Table Ronde, Turin, May 1967, reprinted in *New Scientist*, 2nd June 1967.

the technology of the oceans with its promise of minerals and food supplies. This is certainly one possibility.

This is not the place, however, for the consideration of priorities in terms of projects. The important factor is to make sure that the use of resources, particularly of qualified manpower, is such as to bring about the modernisation of British industry and the British economy. The Labour Government has decided that this can best be done by setting up a number of institutions operating in or in conjunction with the Department of Economic Affairs, the Ministry of Technology, and the Ministry of Education and Science. A great deal of emphasis has been laid on the need to improve on traditional methods of administration both in the official and the private sector. Criticisms of this kind were made in *Conditions Favourable to Faster Growth*, published by the N.E.D.C. under the Conservative Government, and later and in more detail in the National Plan. The responsibilities of governments for the lack of progress made by the economy and for the success or failure of efforts to change the structure are now very widespread indeed. The State is now the manager of the nation's resources in a very real sense. The days have long gone by when the role of Government was regarded as being to keep the ring between management and workers and leave the private enterprise system to produce the right results through the operation of the market. At the present time management and trade unions are brought into consultation with Government in order to secure policy objectives which the Government has laid down. The operation is a political one in which important decisions are political decisions and the policies decided are Party policies. The relationship between Government and Industry has been called 'a course of consultation by condescension'.[1] There will clearly be a long way to go before the modernisation of the British economy is achieved if the system continues to rely for supporting arguments on attributing all the virtues to one political party and all the vices to the other.

[1] John Davies, Director General, C.B.I., Sir George Earle Memorial Lecture, 13th December 1966, reprinted *Three Banks Review*, January 1967.

VIII
The Prices and Incomes Policy

In the years since the war successive governments in Britain have pursued economic policies whose aims were not always consistent one with another. They have at the same time fostered over-full employment while hoping for stable prices. They have failed to resist inflation but have insisted all the time on maintaining a fixed exchange rate for the pound. They have tolerated industrial inefficiency but expected exports to grow. More recently governments have striven for growth at any price and hoped that the balance of payments position would take care of itself. Meanwhile, the electorate has demanded lower taxation but voted for more Government spending on social services and other objects. Sooner or later the moment had to arrive when it was realised that full employment, price stability and free collective bargaining are inconsistent objectives. The obvious solution to this problem is to give up one of the objectives and it is on these grounds that an incomes policy has been advocated at intervals in the post-war period. This amounts to limiting the exercise of free collective bargaining and modifying changes in other incomes so that the sacrifices, if any, fall more or less evenly on incomes from labour and property and on employers and workers. However, it is difficult to put limits on the system of free collective bargaining without introducing modifications elsewhere in the system. So long as there is over-full employment, or demand for resources at current prices is ahead of supply, then price stability is impossible. At this point politicians have to think about levels of employment that are acceptable to the electorate and at the same time effectively to remove the threat to the stability of the economy.

A voluntary restraint on incomes has been a recurring theme in economic policy since 1947. For the most part the period up to 1961, when Mr. Selwyn Lloyd called for a pay pause, was one of exhortation in a vacuum. The severe deflationary measures introduced in July 1961 were followed by a number of steps including the White Paper on *Incomes Policy: the Next Steps* (Cmnd. 1626, February 1962), the setting up of the National Incomes Commission ('Nicky') and the establishment of the National Economic Development Council. The National Incomes Commission never really got off the ground as it failed to secure the support of the T.U.C. The fact that the trade unions agreed to nominate members to the N.E.D.C. went some way to offset this difficulty.

An incomes policy is intended, either as an end in itself or as a condition of faster growth, to keep prices stable. For this to happen unit costs, as the constituents of final prices, must rise no faster than productivity as a whole. However, it is technically extremely difficult to keep final prices steady if indirect taxes— Purchase Tax, taxes on beer, cigarettes and so on—are used as an instrument of stabilisation policy or to redistribute incomes. At the same time prices may rise in a country like Britain with a large foreign trade, because the cost of imports has gone up. All this means that the formulation of precise targets, and the taking of decisions about exactly which prices are going to be stabilised, is extremely difficult. As an exporting nation we should be doing very well if we could be sure of keeping export costs roughly in line with those of our competitors. However, this would mean that policy decisions would depend on what was happening elsewhere and these are the most difficult kind to explain to electors. It is on the whole, therefore, considered better to aim at reasonable stability of prices at home and to make other modifications in economic policy to deal with the balance of payments.

Two important dates in the development of incomes policy in Britain are July 1961 and July 1966, the first representing the end of the period of exhortation and the second the end of voluntary restraint. The importance of Mr. Selwyn Lloyd's measures of 1961 was that for the first time the problem was attacked on several fronts. The policy was in two stages, the first the 'pause' moved away from the arguments which had been put forward by various reports by the 'Three Wise Men' that the basic cause of inflation was the pressure of demand. The 'pause' was not particularly effective in preventing increases of wages in the private sector but hit salaries in the public sector. An increase in wages in the nationalised electricity industry awarded in the autumn of 1961 considerably undermined the effectiveness of the 'pause' and drew complaints from the Chancellor in public speeches. The 'pause' was followed in the second half of 1961 by the 'guiding light' for wage increases which came into operation when the 'pause' ended on 1st April 1962. The 'guiding light' was an attempt to set a limit to the rate of annual wage increases for the economy as a whole. This was calculated at 2·5 per cent for increases in earned incomes. In the accompanying White Paper the Government argued that in the immediate future wages should not as in the past automatically rise with the cost of living. As a part of the incomes policy the Government reaffirmed its intention that 'appropriate corrections would have to be taken if aggregate profits showed signs of increasing excessively as compared with wages and salaries'.[1]

The National Incomes Commission was set up in July 1962 as a body to which all claims concerning remuneration or other conditions of work, except those of the nationalised industries and professions with arbitration machinery, could be referred. As we have seen, the Commission was not supported by the trade unions so that its rate of achievement was low. It served the useful purpose, however, of high-lighting 'wage drift' as an aspect of the incidence of rising money-wages in industry. 'Wage drift' means the difference between hourly earnings excluding overtime and the hourly wage rates arrived at as the result of wage negotiations and collective agreements. This drift is particularly noticeable in engineering, construction, shipbuilding and the electricity industries. Other measures

[1] *Incomes Policy: the Next Steps* (Cmnd. 1926, 1962).

taken by the Conservative Government to limit increases in prices and profits were taken in the spring of 1964. These were the publication of a White Paper on monopolies which was produced as a basis for future legislation in the event of the Conservative Government been returned to power, and a measure to reduce the scope of Resale Price Maintenance was passed in July 1964.

The reports published by the N.E.D.C. in the period before the October 1964 General Election have little to say about prices and incomes. The most important statement was contained in *Conditions Favourable to Faster Growth*. This analysed Britain's export performance in the ten years to 1962 and stated that an important reason for our poor showing was 'the relatively rapid rise in our export prices compared with those of our competitors'. The report pointed out that wage costs per unit of output in British manufacturing industry had risen on average about 3 per cent per annum faster than those of our competitors between 1953 and 1961. This was partly because wage earnings in Britain rose from 1 to 1·5 per cent per annum faster while productivity in British industry rose from 1·5 to 2 per cent per annum more slowly than was the case with our competitors. The N.E.D.C. argument was that with the 4 per cent growth programme productivity in manufacturing should rise at least 1 per cent faster per annum than in the past. On the incomes side the 4 per cent growth programme was based on an increase of about 3·25 per cent in output per head. If the general price level was to remain broadly constant therefore money incomes per head would have to rise at approximately this rate. The report concluded that 'even if rising prices abroad permitted a slow increase in our general price level, rise in money incomes would have to be substantially less rapid than the past average of 5 to 6 per cent a year'. For this to happen there would be a need 'for policies to ensure that money incomes (wages, salaries, profits) as a whole rise substantially less rapidly than in the past'. The report concluded that 'a policy for prices and money incomes can succeed only if those concerned are convinced that it is a necessary part of a wider programme of growth of real incomes, and that restraint by one section of the community will not merely result in a gain by other sections. The Council regards the solution of the difficult problems involved as a necessary part of its task.'[1]

As in other aspects of economic policy the Conservative Government had done little more than re-examine the position and initiate new measures which had not had time to take effect by the time of the General Election in October 1964. The new Government got down to the task of setting up a prices and incomes policy at once. Aided by a large measure of trade union support for its new initiatives, and the rearrangement of the machinery for the conduct of economic policy which had taken place the Government hoped to succeed where their predecessors failed. The first issue of the D.E.A. *Progress Report* (January 1965) led with an introduction by the First Secretary of State, Mr. George Brown, who stated that:

the major results so far (that is, after three months in office) has been the Joint Statement of Intent on Productivity, Prices and Incomes, which—for the first time ever—signals agreement between the Government, employers' associations and the T.U.C. on the strategy for creating a dynamic and socially just Britain. This is a truly historic achievement, which puts Britain in the first rank of countries seeking solutions to the basic problems of an industrial society. I am confident that we can build on this foundation and get practical results. And not only because of the passages in the Joint Statement on a Prices and Incomes Policy—important though that is. I place even higher the undertaking by Management and Unions in paragraph 10 of the Joint Statement: "To encourage and lead a sustained attack on the obstacles to efficiency, whether on the part of Management or of workers, and to strive for the adoption of rigorous standards of performance at all levels. . . ." '

This statement was in line with declarations made during the General Election campaign and with the final resolution of the Annual Conference of the Labour Party in October 1963 which had called for 'an incomes policy covering salaries,

[1] *Conditions Favourable to Faster Growth*, Section G, pages 48–51.

wages, dividends, profits and social security benefits'. The argument was that in contrast to the Conservatives, the Labour Party could appeal for wage restraints because it would at the same time be ensuring that profits and salaries bore their full share of the sacrifice called for.

The Prices and Incomes Policy was to be carried out in three stages. The first was the signature of the Declaration of Intent jointly by representatives of Government, management and the trade unions. The second was an agreement by the parties concerned on the machinery needed to carry the policy out; and finally, the setting of norms for its operation. The timetable for putting these stages into operation was a tight one, but thanks to the energy of Mr. George Brown all three had been achieved by the spring of 1965. The Declaration of Intent was an important advance on what had been done by the Conservative Government in so far as it was the first time that employers and trade unions had come together and voluntarily taken up a common position on prices and incomes. The three aims of the Declaration were to secure an efficient and competitive industry, the growth of incomes within the limits of increasing productivity, and stability of the general price level. The signatories undertook to assist measures to improve productivity, and to co-operate with the Government in the setting up of the machinery needed to put the programme into practice.

In February 1965 the White Paper (*Machinery of Prices and Incomes Policy*—Cmnd. 2577) was published. This began by referring to the Joint Statement of Intent and went on to describe the machinery for keeping the general movement of prices and money incomes of all kinds under review. It pointed out that 'the ascertainment and interpretation of the relevant facts' would require considerable statistical and economic expertise, as well as 'complete impartiality'. This task was handed over to the N.E.D.C. and the results were to be embodied in periodical reports from the N.E.D. Office to the Council. The latter would in turn review the reports submitted to it and consider their implications for the national interest. In other words, N.E.D.C. would be responsible for what the White Paper described as 'ascertainment, interpretation and assessment of the relevant facts about general prices and income behaviour'.

The investigation of particular cases of price and income behaviour called for rather different treatment. The White Paper stated that the Government having discussed with management and unions the problems involved, now proposed to set up under Royal Warrant a National Board for Prices and Incomes, working in two separate divisions to be known as the Prices Review Division and the Incomes Review Division. In practice, the Board has found these two aspects of cases referred to it too closely linked to be separated. The Board consists of an independent chairman, a number of independent members, a businessman and a trade unionist. Between them the members need, according to the White paper, 'expertise in law, accountancy, economics, industrial relations and other relevant fields'. Mr. Aubrey Jones, a former Conservative Minister, with important business connections, was appointed Chairman of the Board.

The third element in the prices and incomes policy, the setting out of the laws to serve as a basis for the work of the National Board for Prices and Incomes, appeared in a White Paper (*Prices and Incomes Policy*—Cmnd. 2659, April 1965). At this time the National Plan was in active preparation and the assumptions for the growth of the economy on which it was based were used in calculating the long-term annual rate of growth of national production per head of the working population. As a result the White Paper decided that an average annual rate of growth of output per head 'of something approaching $3\frac{1}{2}$ per cent' was possible for the years between 1964 and 1970. This was qualified by the statement that 'during the early years of the Plan period the underlying rate of growth will inevitably be below the average for the period as a whole' and continued with the view that 'the rate of increase may be slowed down by reductions in working hours and extended holidays'.

The White Paper set out four sets of circumstances in which exceptional pay increases might be granted. These were:

1. Where the employees concerned, for example, by accepting more exacting work, or a major change in working practices, make a direct contribution towards increasing productivity in the particular firm or industry. Even in such cases some of the benefit should accrue to the community as a whole in the form of lower prices.

2. Where it is essential in the national interest to secure a change in the distribution of manpower (or to prevent a change which would otherwise take place) and a pay increase would be both necessary and effective for this purpose.

3. Where there is general recognition that existing wage and salary levels are too low to maintain a reasonable standard of living.

4. Where there is widespread recognition that the pay of a certain group of workers has fallen seriously out of line with the level of remuneration for similar work and needs in the national interest to be improved.

In practice the norm of 3–3·5 per cent average rate of annual increase in money incomes per head lasted until July of 1966 when the oncoming of the 'freeze' introduced the new concept of a zero norm.

The criteria for price behaviour set out in the White Paper were less specific. It was stated that 'price increases should be avoided where possible and that prices should be reduced wherever circumstances permit'. Exceptions to this general rule were specified and price increases were stated to be acceptable in the following circumstances:

1. If output per employee cannot be raised sufficiently to allow wages and salaries to increase at a rate consistent with the incomes norm without some increase in prices, and no off-setting reductions can be made in non-labour costs per unit of output or in the return sought on investment.

2. There are unavoidable increases in non-labour costs such as raw materials, services or marketing costs per unit of output which cannot be offset by reductions in labour or capital costs or 'in the return sought on investment.'

3. If after every effort has been made to reduce costs, the enterprise is unable to secure the capital required to meet home and overseas demand.

At the same time enterprises were expected to reduce their prices if output per employee was rising faster than the rate of increase in wages and salaries without any off-setting increases in non-labour costs. Reductions were also expected if the cost of raw materials, fuel or services per unit of output were falling, and if the capital costs of output were falling without any off-setting increases in costs. Finally, enterprises were expected to reduce prices in cases where 'profits are based on excessive market power'.

Once the mechanics and objectives of the Prices and Incomes Policy had been settled the next stage was to secure the wider support of the trade unions. The T.U.C. called a conference of the Executive Committees of its affiliated unions on 30th April 1964. This was addressed by Mr. George Brown who stressed the importance of securing increases in real purchasing power rather than paper increases in money incomes. The meeting approved the Government policy by 6·6 million votes against 1·8 million of which 1·4 million votes represented the dissenting voice of the Transport and General Workers' Union. The report published by the T.U.C. on the conference concluded:

The General Council have throughout the discussions made it clear to the Government and to the representatives of the employers' organisations that trade unions would co-operate in a prices and incomes policy only if it appeared to them likely to secure broad trade union objectives more effectively than present policies. They had been guided by the views expressed by Congress that a policy for prices and incomes must be a part of over-all planning: that such a policy would only be acceptable if there was conclusive evidence to show that it was necessary; and that it must include all incomes and allow for the advancement of social equity. The General Council believe that the proposals now put forward meet these requirements and provide the basis for developing a more coherent policy on productivity, prices and incomes.

Although giving their general support to what the Government was trying to do, the trade unions had reservations about accepting a prices and incomes policy as a permanent feature of the economic scene. Mr. George Woodcock, speaking at the Conference, took an extremely realistic view and clearly believed that it would be over-optimistic to expect results in the very near future.

The first references to the Prices and Incomes Board were made by the Government at the beginning of May 1965. The first three were all in respect of prices and dealt with standard bread and the flour used in its manufacture, soap and detergents, and the rates for road haulage as recommended to its members by the Road Haulage Association. The first wages reference concerned the printing industry, clerical workers in the electricity supply industry and the Midland Bank staff salaries. In its first year of operation the Prices and Incomes Board reported on eighteen references and had a further five up for review when its first Annual Report was produced.[1] The reports published by the Prices and Incomes Board have on the whole commanded considerable respect. In the introduction to its first report, that on Road Haulage Rates (Cmnd. 2695) the Board stressed the need for joint action by the Government, by management and by unions in order to secure 'a better reconciliation of the objectives of high employment and faster growth, stable prices and a sounder Balance of Payments'. A distinction was drawn between the possible causes of rising prices. Prices might rise because of a general excess of demand in relation to the capacity to meet it, which might arise from, for example, high level Government spending. The remedy in this case really lay with the Government. Prices might rise equally, however, because of what the report called 'old habits, inherited attitudes and institutional arrangements' which restricted the growth of production, created inflationary pressures and the remedy for which lay with management and trade unions. The ability to take an objective line has been the principal reason for the Board's success. In the General Report it noted that Government action to regulate the economy could give rise to severe pressures on prices which might very well frustrate the intention behind the action taken. It pointed out

[1] National Board for Prices and Incomes General Report, April 1965– July 1966 (Cmnd. 3087).

that in the month in which the Board came into being, that is, April 1965, increases in taxation amounting to £164 million for the year 1965–6 were imposed by the Exchequer. The part of this increase coming from indirect taxes had an immediate effect on prices. One-third of the rise in manufacturers' prices and in retail prices during 1965, according to the report, was due to changes in direct taxation. The object of curtailing demand through increased indirect taxes was frustrated by the Government's inability to control the flow of money. There was nothing to prevent the community from demanding and securing a rise in incomes in order to offset the rise in prices. In the Board's view 'the purpose of the tax increase of April 1965 was frustrated in this way during 1965–6'.

The Second General Report of the Prices and Incomes Board published in August 1967 told a very different story from the first report. During the first period of its operation, May 1965 to July 1966, the Board had been invited to judge references made to it in the light of criteria[1] agreed upon between the Government and the representative organisations of employers and labour. Its recommendations were not legally enforceable and the Board was operating within the framework of a voluntary policy. In the second period, July 1966 to August 1967, the Government imposed a standstill on all wage, price and dividend increases subject to a few very limited exceptions. These exceptions were wider during the period of 'severe restraint' as the second half of the period was called. The Board was not, therefore, in its second year operating rules which were the result of an agreement between Government, management and labour. Its task was now limited to passing judgements only in the light of the exceptions to the standstill laid down by the Government. There was a further difference in that under part four of the Prices and Incomes Act 1966, the Government could enforce any finding put forward by the Board, although it did not in fact do so. With the passing of the Prices and Incomes Act, 1967, which came into force on the 12th August, the Board was again operating on something like its original terms. The big difference, however, was that Govern-

[1] See Appendix VI.

ment, T.U.C. and the C.B.I. had agreed to a 'nil norm'. Under the old criteria, exceptions from the standard wage increase or 'norm' of 3 to 3½ per cent were allowed. The Government now retained a delaying power which in effect enabled it to hold up a proposed pay increase for as long as seven months subject to reference to the Board.

The Second General Report of the Prices and Incomes Board attempted to clarify the position under which the Board operated and the case for giving it enlarged responsibilities. In particular the report posed the question of whether its future role should be simply in the direction of a more permissive attitude to individual wage and price increases or should be towards a comprehensive economic strategy for raising real income based on stable prices and rising productivity. It is difficult if not impossible for the Board to take an intelligent view of individual cases referred to it except as part of an integrated economic policy.

The report pointed out that the role of a productivity prices and incomes policy is to help secure a greater stability of prices for both internal and external reasons. An incomes policy, the report argued, is not inimical to a policy to promote growth but designed to facilitate it. It requires an operation on two fronts, namely the boosting of industrial productivity, and at the same time holding incomes within expanded output limits.

In assessing the Board's place in the national economic and administrative machinery the report examines its relationship with other governmental bodies and with the Government itself. Clearly an organisation such as the Prices and Incomes Board has to fit into an existing administrative structure. Chief among the bodies whose work overlaps or conflicts with the Board's are the Wages Councils. The problem according to the Prices and Incomes Board is twofold. First Wages Councils are required by the Wages Councils Act of 1959 to fix minimum remuneration, but are not empowered to take into account broad considerations of productivity, prices and incomes. Again they decide increases in pay for those receiving the statutory minimum although many of the workers in the different industries covered by Wages Councils receive much more than this. Increases based on the statutory minimum are often passed upwards throughout the entire scale of the industry so that all differentials are correspondingly raised. Wage Councils can, therefore, be pace setters not only in their own industries but in those affected by their activities.

The relationship of the Prices and Incomes Board with the Government falls into three phases—the determination of a reference, the answer to the reference and the action following this answer. The right of determination of references belongs to Government. However, the Board is not an elected body and is therefore concerned mainly with problems of longer-term significance than the Government which is strongly influenced by current public opinion. The Government has encouraged the Board to suggest references which it would regard as appropriate for investigation and according to the report these suggestions have often been taken up. However, it goes on to complain that there is a reluctance on the part of sponsoring departments to see industries under their wings referred to the Board.

At the stage of answering references the Board states that at no time has the Government in any way attempted to influence its findings. On the stage after this it suggests that if its recommendations were disregarded it is open to the Government to refer further aspects of the industry to the Board on a later occasion. As the report remarks it is doubtful whether in the long run an industry could withstand continuous objective exposure to investigation carried out under the public gaze.

The nationalised industries pose a particular problem for the Prices and Incomes Board. In the private sector it is engaged in using price restraint as a form of management discipline. However, in the public sector the Government policy for the nationalised industries is that they should pay their way and earn a prescribed return on capital. This can lead as in the case of electricity and gas to increased prices which have widespread repercussions. It would, of course, be possible for the nationalised industries to opt out of the prices policy on the grounds that their performance is already subject to government scrutiny. Although this policy could be defended it can scarcely be regarded as politically credible. Alternatively the criteria for judging the performance of the nationalised industries can be widened. The return on capital is not by itself an adequate and complete yardstick and needs to be backed up by other forms of discipline relating to costs and prices. This has been recognised by the Prime Minister in the reference to the Prices and Incomes Board of proposed price increases for electricity, gas, the Post Office, London Transport and railway fares. The difficulty is that nationalised industries are very much a special case. Provided projects are likely to yield some benefit over a period of time, investment in them by the Government is regarded as legitimate. This is the case with the nuclear power stations programme and with the Concorde.

The whole question of planning as carried out by the Wilson Government is closely bound up with the way in which the Prices and Incomes Board operates. If the arguments put forward in the Second General Report are accepted its role is certainly very much wider than that of the piecemeal backing of individual wage and price increases. Its responsibilities are enlarged to the point where it becomes an integral part of the planning machinery. While it is clearly desirable for the Board to be able to judge the cases referred to it in as broad a context as possible the fact remains that the Board is not an elected body. Certainly this means that it is free from political and industrial pressures but it is for this very reason that doubts about the wisdom of giving too great a policy-making role to a non-representative body arise.

The difficulties of the Prices and Incomes Board arise from the *ad hoc* nature of the Government's planning. Like the National Economic Development Council before it the Board has come into being with a limited role which has gradually been extended in practice, while the role of the Department of Economic Affairs which brought it into being has changed. What must be recognised in this part of the planning labyrinth is that Government must retain responsibility to Parliament for the general strategy of its economic policy. It can consult with other bodies continuously or from time to time, but the responsibility rests with it. If the Prices and Incomes Board or any other body is to have the role of an independent arbitrator this must be not at the point of initiation of new principles but as an umpire whose function is confined to saying whether a particular case accords or not with the general rules laid down and agreed by Parliament. In the case of the Prices and Incomes Board the position was perfectly clear so long as the 'freeze' operated. The Prices and Incomes Board has done extremely valuable work and its reports[1] are models of clarity and common sense. It should not, however, be in the position where it decides on the content of economic policy.

This still is and must be the role of Parliament.

Events following the devaluation of the pound in November 1947 and the reorganisation of the Cabinet in April 1968 have on the whole strengthened this view. The pattern of responsibility between departments involved in initiating and implementing economic policy has changed with the D.E.A. moving down the scale and the Treasury regaining, many would say reasserting, its dominant position. Responsibility for the prices and incomes policy passed from the D.E.A. to the re-vamped Ministry of Labour—retitled Ministry of Employment and Productivity. The importance of this task was recognised by the fact that Mrs. Barbara Castle, its new head, became First Secretary of State, a title previously held by Mr. Brown and Mr. Stewart when they were in charge of the D.E.A. The post-devaluation phase of the prices and incomes policy requires a 'go slow' on wage increases, while some prices will have to rise to ensure that resources are used for exports rather than domestic consumption. In such a situation emphasis on productivity bargaining is important, but it would be wishful thinking to suppose that any very considerable benefit can be secured from this quarter, or that the prices and incomes policy can be carried on without greatly increased political tensions.

---

[1] See Appendix VII for a list of P.I.B. reports.

IX
Planning and Industry

Although the initiative in economic planning in Britain in the last decade has come from Government, the part played by industry has been of considerable importance. The whole N.E.D.C. operation was made possible by the co-operation of the trade unions and industrial management. This co-operation has raised a number of difficult problems. The structure of the organisations by which management was represented has been reorganised to produce the Confederation of British Industry. This kind of reorganisation was not necessary in the case of the trade unions. However, both were faced with a series of dilemmas. Members of management organisations and the trade unions are appointed by their organisations to represent them on various planning bodies whether Economic Development Committees, Regional Councils or *ad hoc* working parties. Will they be given sufficient freedom to enable them to make effective decisions? If members do not serve as representatives, then they will be liable to be disowned if the conclusions are not acceptable to their organisations. Are there, in fact, built-in pressures towards non-decisions and conformity? Does the weakness of economic planning lie in a lack of understanding about how the economy works? Or is its main defect the lack of communication between Government and industry? Again is economic planning handicapped by deeply ingrained prejudices about what Government should or should not do rather than by a failure to decide what the correct economic policy should be?

The period since the 20th July 1966, which effectively put

an end to the period during which the emphasis on economic policy was on faster growth, has seen considerable discussion about the value of planning. One commentator went so far as to say that:

Not only did the particular 'Plan' of a particular Government come to an end on 20 July, the experiment begun by the National Economic Development Council in 1962 with the object of raising the nation's growth rate, and endorsed by successive Governments of both main political parties, suffered a resounding defeat. One particular approach to economic policy had lost its credibility in this country for the rest of this decade and probably beyond.[1]

It does not follow, however, that the various changes in the machinery of Government affecting economic policy, and a wide range of measures concerning the management of the economy, have all been in vain. Certainly economic forecasting and target-making has not gained any great credit in the last few years. The move towards economic planning, ineffective though it has been, is a recognition of the need for change in the structure of the economy and in attitudes towards economic policy. No one would deny that considerable changes in the structure of the British economy are needed and if planning is regarded as a means of making change less chaotic than it otherwise would be, then planning in some form is likely to be a feature of economic policy for many years to come.

The disenchantment with forecasting and targetry has led to a renewed emphasis on policies to improve economic performance, competitive power and efficiency in the economy. In a letter to *The Times* on 10th April 1967 Sir Robert Shone drew attention to the fact that the identification of obstacles to quicker growth had been a major objective of the N.E.D.C. when it was formed in 1962. The attempt to find a way of bridging the two-way gap between theory and action had been given the name of 'Applied Economics' by Sir Roy Harrod.[2] It was the co-operation between Government, trade unions and

[1] Sam Brittan, 'Inquest on Planning in Britain', *Planning*, January 1967.
[2] See 'The problems of planning for economic growth in a mixed economy', by Sir Robert Shone, *Economic Journal*, Vol. LXXV, March 1965.

management which made it possible for this new approach to be undertaken. Although the results achieved still leave much to be desired, a very considerable improvement in communication has taken place. Looking to the future there is a widespread belief that although Government has a vital part to play in securing the conditions for faster economic growth, and better performance generally, any permanent solution of our problems must come from the development and growth of British industry. This means that the new forms of co-operation which had their beginning in the N.E.D.C. and the Economic Development Committees must be strengthened and made more effective.

The attitudes of trade unions and management to this problem of securing structural change are similar without by any means coinciding. The trade union view has not changed very considerably since the publication of its report on 'Economic Development and Planning' published as Supplementary Report A of the General Council's Report to the 1963 Congress. This stated that 'change in itself does not guarantee economic progress and the change must be consciously directed'. At the same time the report stated that although more accurate co-ordinated economic forecasting was needed, 'forecasting by itself does not provide an automatic corrective for economic deficiencies'. For this planning was needed based on the identification of factors making for change and agreement on objectives and priorities, and establishing the institutional arrangements. This report was published at a time when the N.E.D.C. was still in its early stages. The decision to form some 'systematic consultative arrangements with the major industries' —what in fact became the Economic Development Committees—had already been taken. In the view of the T.U.C. report it was desirable that the new bodies should have 'an element of independence and constructive criticism'. Their aim should be 'to settle problems within the industry but ultimately . . . to draw attention to the problems they cannot solve and make recommendations for action'. Hopes were expressed that the Commissions might become 'a focus for co-operative research and marketing activities or, in time, accumulate or be entrusted with funds for promoting industrial rationalisation'. The first part of this suggestion—the carrying out of research—has become a regular function of the Economic Development Committees. The second task has been handed over to the Industrial Reorganisation Corporation.

The T.U.C. report drew attention to one of the serious difficulties facing the trade unions. At that stage, and this is still true today, providing representatives for all the various planning bodies imposed a considerable strain on union resources. This is not only the problem of selecting the right representatives but also of developing 'technical equipment and methods of communication'. The question of communication has been extremely important in the planning process. The need for adequate means of channelling information down to and up from rank and file members is clearly necessary, 'if working people are to feel that they have a share in planning'.

In an unusually prescient section on the Implications for Trade Unionists the report stated that

planning is unlikely to solve all Britain's problems, nor will it eliminate all differences of view between industry and the Government or between trade unionists and employers. It should however perhaps clarify those differences and establish a framework within which agreement can be reached by negotiation and compromise. Planning should in particular create conditions of economic expansion in which employers and trade unionists can more easily settle their common problems. It will also create problems for the trade union movement.

This judgement has been borne out in practice, particularly in the experience of the working of the Prices and Incomes Policy. The position of the trade unions under a Labour Government is somewhat different from under a Conservative one. Although the T.U.C. co-operated with the Macmillan Government in the setting up of the N.E.D.C., it refused to participate in the National Incomes Council which preceded it. Because of its close institutional links with the Labour Party the trade union movement is in general terms more likely to accept unpleasant measures passed by a Labour rather than a Conservative Government. However, as events have shown, it is possible for a powerful trade union to oppose a major item of Government policy as the Transport and General Workers' Union has done over the Prices and Incomes Policy.

Although the trade unions have still a very long way to go before their structure can be regarded as equal to the role they have to play in our economic life, there is no doubt that a great deal has been done to modernise them in the last decade. In some respects the General Council of the T.U.C. shoulders responsibilities which are greater than the powers at its disposal. This is particularly the case with the representatives of the General Council on the N.E.D.C. A Royal Commission on Trade Unions and Employers' Associations was set up in February 1965. Its terms of reference were 'to consider relations between management and employees and the role of trade unions and employers' associations in promoting the interests of the members and in accelerating the social and economic advance of the nation with particular reference to the law affecting the activities of these bodies'. The fact remains that the task of the trade unions is an extremely difficult one and many of the shortcomings that the movement displays have causes outside the immediate control of union officials.

Governments have the means and power to govern. Management has the means, power and training to improve productivity. The trade unions are voluntary societies with scarcely any sanction except the personal authority of their union leaders. Their whole training is to claim higher wages: they can hardly recommend lower wages than managements competing for labour are prepared to concede. While managements are busy bidding to attract labour away from each other, the union leader's job is exceptionally difficult.[1]

The difficulties of trade union members of statutory bodies are illustrated by the case of Mr. Robert Willis, Joint General Secretary of the National Graphical Association, who became

[1] H. F. R. Catherwood, *Britain with the Brakes Off*, Hodder & Stoughton, 1966.

a full-time member of the National Board for Prices and Incomes on its foundation. As a full-time member, a trade unionist receives a salary probably at least double what his union paid him and, if he is on leave of absence, he is able to return to his former post in due course. However, if he is away from union work for a long period, he loses touch with developments within his old union and comes to be regarded as a 'Government' man. Part-time membership of official bodies is not nearly such a good proposition for trade unionists as for industrialists. The latter can often find the time to serve on a Board or Committee but would find the full-time pay too small. Trade unionists would find part-time membership of a body which was taking decisions unpopular with their colleagues an extremely difficult proposition. They would run into difficulties particularly when they came to seek re-election in their posts or election to higher union office. So long as Governments select trade union leaders at the height of their power and influence, rather than elderly nonentities to serve on official bodies, this dilemma will persist.

The proposition that economic planning is more likely to be handicapped in the future by deeply engrained prejudices about what Governments should or should not do rather than by our inability to determine what correct economic policy should be, applies equally to management. Whatever views we may hold about planning as it has operated in the last decade, there is no doubt that with the growing complexity of the economic system there is little chance of doing better in the future unless we are willing to face a certain amount of intervention. There is no point in pretending that the free-market system is in operation in this country and it is extremely doubtful that if by some miracle the State could be made to take up a neutral position in relation to industry, that we should be able to achieve a higher rate of performance in the economy. Getting rid of the controls and devices by which Governments influence industry would mean changing the system of taxation, the social services, the operation of the public sector, Government investment direct and indirect, legislation on regional policy and on town and country planning, education and training and so on. To say this does not mean that we must accept the present paraphernalia of economic policy as being the best that can be devised. Technological innovation has gone a long way towards providing the means by which problems of production can be solved more quickly and with less effort. But, so far, we have failed to find ways and means of taking advantage of these possibilities through inability to regulate the economy and prevent the operation of the dreary stop-go cycle.

This situation has led to a variety of conclusions. Professor John Jewkes[1] has stated that

the moral to be drawn is not highly complicated; nor is it dependent upon complex and highly sophisticated economic analysis. It is simply that the cure for bad planning of this type is not better planning but no planning. The prospects of improvements in the standard of living of people will be more favourable if we drop the belief that by thinking of numbers, we can do much to improve our lot. The wiser course for any government to follow is to do whatever it can to create a general environment conducive to growth and then leave the rate of growth to settle itself, recognising that this is a highly unpredictable world and that to tie oneself to one figure is likely to be more embarrassing than helpful.

How to decide ways and means of creating a general environment conducive to growth has baffled successive Governments. A proposal from a group of economists and writers published in July 1967 came to the conclusion that the priorities for Government action centred around 'the two main instruments of economic management', namely, monetary policy and fiscal policy. The detailed implementation of the proposals included the cutting of Government expenditure on a basis that would ensure that public sector spending could only increase in relation to the growth of the private sector. Other proposals dealt with the need to set up an independent consultancy organisation to appraise the cost-effectiveness of Government departments with a view to reducing the number of civil servants and the cost of Government; the gradual reduction of all subsidies; a recasting of the tax system and 'genuine consul-

[1] *The New Ordeal By Planning*, Macmillan, London, 1968.

133

tation between Government and industry before far-reaching decisions are taken'.[1]

Exactly when consultation between Government and industry becomes 'genuine' is difficult to say. An examination of the ways in which Government is involved with industry was carried out by Mr. John Davies, the Director General of the Confederation of British Industry, in the Sir George Earle Memorial Lecture.[2] Mr. Davies pointed out that Government is involved with industry in six different ways. The first is as protector of the people by keeping the peace, preventing industry from harming the interests of others by polluting the air or water, invading their privacy and recreation, upsetting their rights as customers by using excessive market power, treating them harshly as workpeople, and harming their interests as shareholders. Secondly, Government acts as a provider of services of a variety of kinds, such as post and tele-communications, transport, health, police, fuel and power, education, labour and employment services. Thirdly, the State appears as a customer, spending 40 per cent of the Gross National Product and in the process coming into contact with every sector of industry and commerce. Fourthly, as the proprietor of the nationalised industries, the State is itself an industrialist, competing with private industry for customers and resources and dealing with the same sort of industrial problems as private concerns. Fifthly, the Government is responsible for the framework of trading agreements in which industry operates, as well as for the impact on these of foreign organisations. Finally, the Government is the manager of the nation's resources, a function which affects everyone.

In this last role Mr. Davies believes that Government 'can and will henceforward use its powers for the apportionment of resources in line with its social policy'. Governments have been following this role for a generation or more and it has been broadly accepted, provided that it is carried out competently.

[1] 'A programme for National Recovery', Sponsoring Committee of the National Recovery Programme, July 1967. Among those signing were Graham Hutton, Professor Northcote Parkinson, Colin Clark, Sir Arthur Bryant, Sir Halford Reddish and Lord Aberdare.
[2] Reprinted as 'Industry and Government', *Three Banks Review*, June 1967.

'As far as industry is concerned, competence is seen,' by Mr. Davies, 'as consistency and comprehensibility adding up to a stimulating and stable economic framework within which enterprise can flourish without undue interference.' While many businessmen see this as a correct relationship between Government and industry, a new factor has already entered the situation. This is the belief by Governments in the last decade that it is not enough to appropriate and apportion resources and safeguard the interests of individuals but that it also has 'a leading part to play in the *creation* of national resources'. This has meant that Government has increasingly taken part in the struggle for higher production. This has led to the building up of 'a veritable maze of consultative groupings conceived with dual objective of genuinely acquiring knowledge of the workings of industry on the one side and, on the other, of quietening fears that may be preparing to act in an arbitrary or impulsive manner'.

This is, indeed, the problem facing management. There is the need for a greatly increased flow of information about the working of the economic system. Communication between management and trade unions and between Government and both is necessary. New ways of analysing and assessing the performance of the economic system are essential. But when it comes down to putting all these together in the 'new applied economics' experience shows that the effort of securing the bold forward sweep of the economy is full of difficulties. Industrial management at first greeted the prospect of co-operating in economic policy-making as a means of securing a better working of the economy. However, not the least problem that has emerged is the fact that highly centralised planning can be extremely wasteful of ability. The 'veritable maze of consultative groupings' is, to say the least, time consuming and represents a great diversion away from normal business pursuits.

The C.B.I. complaint, according to Mr. Davies, is that all this effort does not represent the Government 'genuinely trying to understand the industrial world'. The Government is not trying to 'improve and refine' the framework within which private enterprise operates, it is itself 'getting in on the act'.

What is happening is that Government is now 'isolating the individual strands of the texture of industry and seeking to strengthen or weaken them as its own convictions of what was good for them demanded'. The difficulty about this is that it is not in the nature of Governments to understand how industry operates. The whole system is too complicated and diverse for this.

What can be done to make the preparation and implementation of economic policy more effective? The C.B.I., like the T.U.C., has made great efforts to carry its members with it in co-operating with both Conservative and Labour Governments in the planning process as it has developed. Indeed, the setting up of the C.B.I. by the process of amalgamating the existing management organisations was a part of this process. When Mr. Davies said that the Government is 'getting in on the act' itself he was voicing the fear that consultation may increase rather than reduce the area of misunderstanding between Government and industry. There are echoes here of the statement by Mr. Robert Willis in his letter of resignation addressed to Mr. Michael Stewart, Minister of Economic Affairs, on leaving the Prices and Incomes Board (see page 131) of a growing gulf between Ministers and the Board. What had started as a voluntary operation with the Declaration of Intent had produced in Mr. Willis's view a body which was no longer independent 'within the framework of Statutory Legislation but merely the servant of certain Ministers'.[1]

The way out of this dilemma, according to Mr. John Davies, is to replace consultation by partnership. Consultation implies a willingness of Government to listen to what management and trade unions have to say. It does not imply any obligation to reach a decision based on the views of all three parties. As Mr. Davies says, 'it is a process that risks making enemies rather than friends'. At the same time, partnership, meaning the sharing of the power of decision, is an extremely difficult concept for Governments to accept. It means, for example, the discussion of tax measures before these are framed and presented to Parliament. The experience of the Selective Employment

[1] See *The Times*, 29th July 1967.

Tax, which was bitterly opposed by the C.B.I., is very relevant here. The assumption that it was possible to shift workers from the service industries into production by a single fiscal measure was regarded by the C.B.I. as ludicrous, and the nature of the administrative arrangements affecting this with their cumbersome system of collecting money from everybody and returning different amounts to different categories of industry made the whole exercise absurd. A system which makes it possible for the Chancellor to announce a measure of this kind without warning is not surprisingly distrusted by all sections of industry.

Partnership would mean very radical changes in Government procedures, and would also involve sacrifices by management. If Governments are to reveal their intentions to industry then businessmen must expect to be required to disclose far more of their own activities than they have in the past. The right to make decisions with consideration solely for the individual enterprise can hardly be sustained. In a society as complex as that of the United Kingdom it is difficult to introduce the kind of sweeping changes in procedures and attitudes which would make possible a system of partnership enabling joint consideration to be given to all government and industrial actions relating to the use of resources. However, unless the parties to the discussion, Government, management and trade unions, are prepared to sacrifice some of their sovereignty then the present endless round of discussion without decision and activity without action is likely to continue indefinitely. But is it impossible to think of economic planning divorced from political allegiance? Could partnership between Government and industry produce a national plan which was an 'aggregation of the alternative conclusions reached in discussions aimed at the optimisation of resources'? To some extent, we have now reached a point where the politicians are not divided on planning or not planning but on the type of planning to adopt. If the whole process of consultation is carried forward in depth the result would be to take economic planning, at least in principle, into the area slightly above political discussion which is normally occupied by foreign policy. Anyone who has taken part in the planning process as at present operated, will be well aware of the need for something more effective than consultation. Unless it is brought about there is the danger that relationships between Government and industry, both management and trade unions, will deteriorate because of the frustrations and mistakes of the present system of 'consultation by condescension'.

Are there any signs that a movement in this direction is possible? On the Government side it would be premature to say that the lessons of the past few years have been learnt. The unfavourable reaction of the C.B.I. to the second National Productivity Conference called by the Prime Minister in June 1967 is an indication of this. Sir Stephen Brown, President of the C.B.I., stated[1] that while the Prime Minister described the Conference as 'the Parliament of Industry' and a 'Great Conference' in his view 'there was very grave doubt whether that sort of exercise could achieve the original objects', and participation by the C.B.I. in a further Conference of this kind was regarded as of doubtful value.

But even if 'Great Conferences' on productivity are out, the C.B.I. and T.U.C. have moved some way towards making consultation more effective on this subject. A joint campaign to increase productivity was announced on the 26th July for joint action by the two bodies. The scheme began with an invitation from the C.B.I. to all employees' organisations to discuss with the trade unions what arrangements could be made for consultations with workers at both industry and firm level on the more efficient use of labour. The T.U.C. took the important step of writing to affiliated unions suggesting that they should co-operate in these discussions. Once the industry level consultative arrangements had been agreed the next step would be for employers' organisations to invite member firms to consider new initiatives at company or plant level. The C.B.I. agreed to distribute a list of vital points prepared by the Labour Utilisation Committee of the N.E.D.C. Firms were asked to report back to their employers' organisations or to the C.B.I. on difficulties which continued to restrict the more efficient use of labour, trade union representatives were in

[1] *British Industry*, 7th July 1967.

138

touch on the same lines with their headquarters. Problems that arise will be considered by a joint C.B.I./T.U.C. Steering Committee which will supervise the whole scheme.

At the press conference in London to launch the new scheme,[1] Sir Stephen Brown said: 'We are all thoroughly tired of endless talk and some of us think that there are too many committees.' He went on to emphasise that industrialists were not 'starry-eyed' in expecting dramatic results in the shape of a fresh upsurge in productivity figures. Sir Harry Douglass (now Lord Douglass) said that the scheme was intended to force productivity to the attention of everybody, down to the shop floor. Differences between employers and unions arose when it came to sharing out the results of higher productivity, but there had to be extra profits to hand round. The important feature of this affable understanding is that the T.U.C. and C.B.I. were trying to get beyond declarations of intention and arrive at a practical working relationship. If the C.B.I. and the T.U.C could work together, the N.E.D.C. and the Economic Development Committees and all the rest of the 'veritable maze of consultative groupings' would begin to have some real significance.

[1] See *The Times*, 27th July 1967.

X

Those Corridors of Power

Of all the clichés of present times, the 'corridors of power' has been one of the most overworked. Many businessmen have a deep-rooted scepticism about the power of Governments to bring about fundamental and quick changes in the way that people behave. The idea that Ministers sitting in their offices in Whitehall can take decisions that will suddenly make industry efficient or get rid of some long-standing but unhelpful attitude either in management or trade unions would be regarded with some dubiety in most board rooms. Any government is limited in what it can do by the amount of information it has at its disposal, the ability of its advisers to analyse problems to be solved and the machinery available to it for carrying out its economic policies. The limitations on the first two factors are likely to persist. Although there have been some improvements since Mr. Macmillan complained that working out economic policy on the basis of the statistical information available to him was like trying to catch a train with the help of 'last year's *Bradshaw*', there is no doubt that policy-makers are often working in statistical darkness. The ability of civil servants to understand complicated economic problems and to sort out the priorities correctly has been questioned by a number of writers. One of the most outspoken of these has gone so far as to suggest that the Treasury should be abolished as an essential step in securing better administration.[1] In the last few years the efforts of the career civil servants have been supplemented by businessmen and others on secondment from outside. While this has meant that new points of view have had

[1] See *The System*, by Max Nicholson, Macmillan, London 1967.

an airing in Whitehall, the extent to which it has been done has necessarily been limited.

In the end the things that any government can do to influence economic policy are by no means numerous. However many new organisations are set up, the prospect that they will produce panaceas can only be regarded as remote. What in fact Governments can do is:

(a) vary the supply of money and therefore the level of demand in the economy;

(b) make use of physical controls to channel activity in particular directions;

(c) set up new agencies which may operate either by securing voluntary agreement of those concerned, or on the strength of powers given to them by Parliament;

(d) exhort the business community and public to follow a particular line of action by means of public relations and its various techniques;

(e) introduce legislation to make people act in a particular way; and

(f) act directly in the public sector, for example, setting output targets for the National Coal Board.

Government policy in the 1960s has consisted of variations on these themes. The emphasis has varied according to which party has been in power and according to the severity of the problems facing particular administrations. The fact that the balance of payments has been a continuing problem has placed severe limits on the freedom of action of Conservative and Labour Governments alike. Both have, at different times, come to the conclusion that it was essential for Britain to join the European Economic Community. In both cases the advantages of a bigger market for British industry have been stressed. It is clearly not possible to go very far in forecasting the future of the British economy without knowing whether or not the United Kingdom will be a part of an extended Common Market. No National Plan which was not able to take account of this eventuality could be regarded as in any way realistic. However, the fact that planning is difficult is not by any means a new discovery. Without entering into any commitment for detailed planning of the kind set out in the National Plan, there is everything to be said for having a series of forward projections based on current policy assumptions as a basis for policy decisions and public debate about them. The process of bringing industrialists and trade unionists into participation in the machinery of Government depends on the creation of an informed body of opinion within industry. The greater the uncertainties to be faced the greater the importance of setting out clearly what the possibilities are and the risks attaching to alternative decisions concerning them. In this sense all large private corporations carry out planning and this is a practice which will increase in volume with the advance of technology. There is always a danger that the appetite of Government for intervention in the economy will outrun its capacity to intervene effectively. It is in the nature of politics that Governments are susceptible to outside pressures and it is these which produce initiatives. It is, therefore, all the more important that businessmen should not only understand the techniques and developments in their own industry, but that they should be able to place these in the wider context in which their own affairs are simply components in the national statistics.

The experience of industry in co-operating with Government in the 1960s has produced a number of lessons. The first is that to be successful, consultation must be continuous. Invitations to dinner at Number 10 may be flattering to the self-esteem of the recipients but they neither solve problems nor indeed bring them much closer to solution. Again successful consultation takes place between people who can commit their members to agreement with the decisions they take. This is one of the critical factors in any planning system that is based on securing the agreement of the planned. Neither the T.U.C. nor the C.B.I. can claim to be able to guarantee the complete compliance of their members in any agreement they reach. A further consideration is the need to inject new ideas into the thinking of consultative bodies. The most lively minds are not always found among representatives of management organisations or the major trade unions. Somehow the knowledge, and where it exists, the wisdom of the scientists, technologists, practising economists and others must be brought into use. Tycoons and trades union leader are alike in not being particularly fertile in seminal ideas. Their strength lies in exploiting the ideas which have already proved successful. One clear lesson that has emerged from the move to introduce some form of planning into the British economy is that institutional change and innovation is a slow process. Existing Government departments are opposed to the setting up of new ones that may encroach on their particular field of operations. The Treasury and Board of Trade were both opposed to the setting up of the Department of Economic Affairs. The members of the N.E.D. Office were not overjoyed at the appearance of industrial advisers in the D.E.A. with closer links with industry than they had. Departments with well-established machinery for co-operation were by no means anxious to see these superseded by some new arrangement. One example of this was the snail's pace at which arrangements for setting up a 'Little Neddy' for agriculture moved forward. The Ministry needed to be convinced that any new body that it might help to create would not upset the Annual Price Review system which had been operating with considerable success. This was not obstructionism but distrust based on the simple belief that Mr. George Brown's decision to have twenty committees set up by a particular target date should not be allowed to disrupt existing arrangements which had proved their usefulness but did not happen to fit into the new pattern.

The new model agencies with their mixture of civil servants, businessmen, academics and other 'irregulars', introduce a number of problems. The 'irregulars' have to learn to understand the strengths and weaknesses of the civil service system. In particular, they must familiarise themselves with the procedures for ensuring that unwanted proposals do not disappear without trace. So long as mixed membership organisations are dealing with economic and commercial problems, the members are able to take account of each other's views without too much difficulty. When they are faced with problems arising out of political decisions the position is different. This happened when the Prime Minister took over the chairmanship of the N.E.D.

Council in October 1967 and proceeded to explain what the Industrial Expansion Bill would do and how it would be introduced. The C.B.I. members protested that objections they had put forward against the bill had not been listened to and discarded. There is clearly a point beyond which representative bodies, whether on the management or trade union sides, cannot go without abandoning the interests of their members. At the same time Governments regard themselves as being elected to implement their Election programmes. When a politically controversial measure comes up for discussion the limitations of planning by consultation and agreement are exposed.

The businessman looking for a way through the planning labyrinth has therefore to keep a number of threads in his hand. One of these is attached to long-term problems of which he must keep informed in the interests of his own company, including questions of export competitiveness, costs and prices. Another leads into the various Government offices dealing with taxation, factory legislation and all the host of regulations that he has to comply with in the conduct of his business. A third thread leads to the organisations concerned with his own industry—the trade associations, productivity councils, training boards and other specialist bodies. This thread leads him beyond the interests of his own business to its relationship with the rest of the industry within which it operates. The next thread leads on to bodies such as the N.E.D.C. and the Little Neddies, where the affairs of his industry are discussed in terms of the wider issues affecting the economy as a whole. At some times these discussions will be concerned with fitting his industry into a long-term growth programme or a national plan. At others they will be directed towards removing obstacles to better performance. Whatever the emphasis, the threads leading up to this level are concerned with planning. At this stage the individual factory has become a component of the national statistics.

There still remain one or two threads which the industrialist will find useful in seeking a path through the planning labyrinth. One of these is marked 'Information' and leads to the press, radio and television, and other sources of opinion, facts and figures. These sources will not tell him what he should be doing at a particular point in time. But they will help him to see his own activities in the wider context of national economic policy. Even if he dislikes what he sees as a result of orientating himself in this way, the businessman will at least have the advantage of knowing where he is and having some idea of where he is likely to be going. Finally, there are a number of coloured threads—different people will select different colours —which lead to the political parties. These on the whole tend to be the least reliable guides through the labyrinth, as their originators are concerned not only in trying to find the right way themselves, but in demonstrating that their rivals are pointing in quite the wrong direction. The pursuit of planning in which industry is now engaged is in danger of becoming a paper-chase in which the competitors are led through a variety of obstacles many of which are not strictly relevant to the problem in hand. Governments have to remember that it is idle to expect businessmen to take risks unless there is a climate of confidence favourable to expansion. And trade unionists cannot be expected to be greatly interested in increasing productivity through changing work schedules or adopting labour-saving procedures at a time of rising unemployment. In other words, attitudes are the hardest thing to change whether they are enshrined in a political manifesto, in a resolution passed by a trade union meeting or in an unshakeable belief that *laissez-faire* is the only possible basis for the economic policy for any Government, no matter what its political complexion.

The pursuit of planning has not so far met with any outstanding successes. The result of the work of a number of the Little Neddies has obviously led to gains in efficiency. The reports of the Prices and Incomes Board have provided a new addition to the analysis of industrial problems. But there have been mistakes such as the too hasty launching of regional planning and the disaster of the National Plan. Nevertheless, the pursuit will go on in one direction or another simply because there is no alternative. What kind of economic policy arrangements we shall have in the 1970s are anybody's guess.

We must hope that they are backed up by better and more up-to-date sources of information than those of today, so that decision-taking is not always a leap in the dark. Again, we do not know what the scale of our industrial base will be—whether we shall be operating in a wider European market, in an Atlantic Community or still just making passes in likely directions. We can only hope that by the time we reach the end of the planning labyrinth we shall have discovered ways and means of formulating and implementing economic policy that will make it possible to operate an economy in which growth does not lead inevitably to a trade deficit and deflation, and where 'stop' and 'go' have no economic significance.

What industry has to fear in the years ahead is not Government interference in the running of the economy, but haphazard interference. The real weakness of the Labour Government was not that its National Plan was a failure, but that the whole basis of its economic policy was inconsistent. Businessmen want to know about the medium-term economic strategy of the Government. For this reason some kind of planning document is likely to be forthcoming from future Governments whatever their complexion. The sort of thing that is likely to be produced will be an attempt to spotlight sectors of the economy where change is taking place, whether from home investment, import substitution or rising exports. In addition trends in production and payments would be forecast as part of a broad guide to the possible direction of structural change. In the early days of the N.E.D.C. it was usual to describe its function as being centralised market research. This is the sort of planning that the experience of the 1960s has shown to be necessary and feasible. Provided the limitations are clearly recognised and the politicians do not try to take over the act by blurring the distinction between forecasts and targets, it should be possible to find a form of activity that was not only acceptable to Government, C.B.I. and T.U.C. but also secured a more effective management of the economy.

The Planning Labyrinth

*The Ministries and Organisations concerned
as on 1 May 1968*

Economic Policy

Cabinet—includes following Ministries dealing with economic
policy
Treasury
Board of Trade
Ministry of Employment and Productivity
Department of Economic Affairs.
Ministry of Transport
Ministry of Technology
Ministry of Power
Ministry of Agriculture

Also deeply involved:
Bank of England—independent of, but working closely with,
the Treasury

New Organisations (post 1960) involved in making and imple-
menting economic policy
National Economic Development Council (of which Prime
Minister is Chairman)
Economic Development Committees (Little Neddies)
Prices and Incomes Board
Industrial Reorganisation Corporation
Regional Economic Councils and Boards

The National Economic Development Council

I. The Council under the Macmillan Government
Chairman: The Chancellor of the Exchequer
Rt. Hon. Selwyn Lloyd—February 1962–July 1963
Rt. Hon. Reginald Maudling—July 1963–October 1964
The President of the Board of Trade
The Minister of Labour

Management (Initial membership as at 8 February 1962)
Mr. F. A. Cockfield, Chairman, Boots Pure Drug Co.
Mr. R. M. Geddes, o.b.e., Managing Director, Dunlop Rubber Co. Ltd.
Sir Cyril Harrison, Vice-Chairman, English Sewing Cotton Co. Ltd.
Sir John Hunter, c.b.e., Chairman, Swan Hunter & Wigham Richardson Ltd.
Mr. J. M. Laing, Managing Director, John Laing & Son Ltd.
Sir John Toothill, c.b.e., Director, Ferranti Ltd.

Trade Unions
Sir William Carron, President, Amalgamated Engineering Union
Mr. F. Cousins, General Secretary, Transport & General Workers' Union
Sir Harry Douglass, General Secretary, Iron and Steel Trades Confederation
Mr. S. F. Greene, General Secretary, National Union of Railwaymen
Mr. R. Smith, General Secretary, Union of Post Office Workers
Mr. G. Woodcock, c.b.e., General Secretary, Trades Union Congress

Independents
The Rt. Hon. Lord Franks, G.C.M.G., K.C.B., C.B.E., Provost of
Worcester College, Oxford
Professor H. Phelps Brown, Professor of the Economics of
Labour, London School of Economics

Nationalised Industries
Dr. R. Beeching, Chairman, British Transport Commission
The Rt. Hon. Lord Robens of Woldingham, Chairman,
National Coal Board

Director General
Sir Robert Shone, C.B.E., Director General of the staff of the
Council

II. The Council under the Wilson Government

Chairman: Minister for Economic Affairs and First Secretary
of State
Rt. Hon. George Brown—October 1964–July 1966
Rt. Hon. Michael Stewart—July 1966–August 1967
The Prime Minister—August 1967–
President of the Board of Trade
Minister of Employment and Productivity
Minister of Technology
Secretary of State for Economic Affairs (since August 1967)
Note: the Chancellor of the Exchequer has attended meetings
of the Council since August 1967

Management
Sir Frank Kearton, Chairman, Courtaulds Ltd.
Mr. John Davies, Director General, Confederation of British
Industry
Mr. John Partridge, Chairman, Imperial Tobacco Co. Ltd.
Mr. K. A. Keith, Deputy Chairman, Hill Samuel & Co.
Sir Stephen Brown, President, Confederation of British
Industry
Mr. A. G. Norman, Chairman, De La Rue Co. Ltd.

L

Appendices

Trade Unions

Mr. George Woodcock, General Secretary, Trades Union Congress

Lord Carron, President, Amalgamated Engineering Union

Mr. S. F. Greene, General Secretary, National Union of Railwaymen

Lord Cooper, General Secretary, National Union of General and Municipal Workers

Mr. F. Cousins, General Secretary, Transport and General Workers' Union

Independents

Professor D. J. Robertson, Department of Social and Economic Research, University of Glasgow

Sir Steuart Mitchell, Chairman of Shipbuilding Industry Training Board

Nationalised Industries

Lord Robens, Chairman, National Coal Board

Sir Ronald Edwards, Chairman, Electricity Council

Chairman, National Board for Prices and Incomes

Rt. Hon. Aubrey Jones

Director General

Mr. H. F. R. Catherwood from May 1966

Sir Robert Shone until May 1966

APPENDIX III

The Economic Development Committees

('Little Neddies')

Dates of Formation and Chairmen

Committee	*Chairman*
Agriculture (22nd December 1966)	Sir Edmund Bacon, B.T., K.B.E., T.D., J.P. Chairman, British Sugar Corporation.
Building (21st June 1965)	Lord Campbell of Eskan, President, Booker Brothers, McConnell and Co. Ltd.
Chemicals (20th April 1964)	Lord Pilkington, Chairman, Pilkington Brothers, Ltd.
Civil Engineering (21st June 1965)	Lord Campbell of Eskan, President, Booker Brothers, McConnell and Co. Ltd.
Clothing (3rd May 1966)	Mr. R. Appleby, Chairman and Managing Director, Black and Decker Ltd.
Distributive Trades (15th July 1964)	Sir Hugh Weeks, C.M.G., Director, Industrial and Commercial Finance Corporation Ltd.

151

Construction Materials Group (8th October 1964)	F. A. Bishop, Whitehall Securities Corporation.
Electrical Engineering (26th May 1964)	Sir Leslie Robinson, K.B.E., C.B., Industrial adviser, J. Henry Schroder Wagg and Co. Ltd., formerly Second Secretary, Board of Trade.
Electronics (23rd April 1964)	Sir Donald Stokes, T.D., Deputy Chairman and Managing Director, Leyland Motor Corporation (to April 1968).
Food Manufacturing (combining former Chocolate and Sugar Confectionery (14th May 1964) and Food Processing E.D.C.s (8th July 1965)	Mr. J. R. M. Rocke, Vice-Chairman, Booker Brothers, McConnell and Co. Ltd.
Hosiery and Knitwear (26th May 1966)	Mr. L. Spalton, Chairman, Sterling Winthrop Group Ltd.
Hotel and Catering (20th June 1966)	Sir William Swallow, K.B., Formerly Chairman, Vauxhall Motors Ltd.
Machine Tools (15th April 1964)	Sir Richard Way, Chairman, Lansing Bagnall Ltd.
Mechanical Engineering (21st May 1964)	Mr. D. A. C. Dewdney, A managing director, Esso Petroleum Co. Ltd.

Motor Manufacturing Industry (30th June 1967)	Sir Hugh Tett, Chairman, Esso Petroleum Co. Ltd.
Motor Vehicle Distribution and Repair (13th October 1966)	Sir John Toothill, C.B.E., Director and General Manager, Ferranti Ltd.
Movement of Exports (21st July 1965)	Viscount Caldecote, D.S.C., Deputy Managing Director, British Aircraft Corporation.
Newspaper, Printing and Publishing (24th January 1966)	Mr. H. R. Mathys, Deputy Chairman, Courtaulds Ltd.
Paper and Board (20th May 1964)	Sir Mark Turner, Deputy Chairman, Kleinwort-Benson Ltd.
Post Office (14th March 1966)	Sir Andrew Crichton, P & O Steam Navigation Company.
Process Plant Working Party (11th August 1966)	Mr. K. M. Leach, Deputy Chairman, Serck Ltd.
Rubber (15th July 1965)	Mr. J. E. Bolton, D.S.C., Formerly Chairman and Managing Director of the Solartron Electronic Group Ltd.
Wool Textiles (25th May 1964)	Mr. W. H. Mosley Isle, Retired partner, Peat, Marwick, Mitchell & Co.

APPENDIX IV

Economic Planning Boards and Councils

Northern Region:	Wellbar House, Gallowgate, Newcastle 1. Tel: Newcastle 27575
Yorkshire & Humberside Region:	City House, Leeds 1. Tel: Leeds 38232
East Midlands Region:	Cranbrook House, Cranbrook Street, Nottingham. Tel: Nottingham 46121
East Anglia Region:	2 Queen Anne's Gate Buildings, Dartmouth Street, London, S.W.1. Tel: TRA 7848
South West Region:	Avon House, Telephone Avenue, Bristol 1. Tel: Bristol 293195
West Midlands Region:	Five Ways House, Islington Row, Birmingham 1. Tel: Midland 8191
North West Region:	Sunley Building, (11th Floor), Piccadilly Plaza, Manchester 1. Tel: Deansgate 9111
Wales:	Welsh Office, Cathays Park, Cardiff. Tel: Cardiff 28066

Scotland:	Scottish Office, St. Andrew's House, Edinburgh 1. Tel: Edinburgh Waverley 8545
South East Region:	Queen Anne's Gate Buildings, Dartmouth Street, London, S.W.1. Tel: TRA 7848
Northern Ireland:	Ministry of Commerce, Chichester House, Chichester Street, Belfast, N.1. Tel: Belfast 28271

APPENDIX V

On the Industrial Front

(a) *Management Organisations*
Confederation of British Industry
(formed 1965 from Federation of British Industry, British Employers Confederation and National Union of Manufacturers)
National Association of British Chambers of Commerce
British Institute of Management
Institute of Directors
Trade Associations
(ranging from federations covering whole industries to small bodies with limited terms of reference. The exact number of these is not known but it is of the order of 1,300)

(b) *Trade Unions*
Affiliated trade unions including general unions, federations of unions, craft unions
There are some 650 trade unions in Britain with a total membership of about 10 millions
Nearly 8 million workers are members of the 38 largest unions
Over 3 million workers are in the three largest unions

APPENDIX VI

Summary of Criteria

The White Paper *Prices and Incomes Policy after June 30, 1967* (Cmnd. 3235), published in March 1967, set out the criteria for prices and incomes decisions during the current phase of the policy.

The continuing aim is to restrain increases in prices and encourage necessary investment. Every effort should be made to absorb increases in costs.

PRICES:

Increases should not take place unless:

(1) output per employee cannot be increased sufficiently to allow wages and salaries to increase at a rate consistent with the criteria for incomes;

(2) there are unavoidable increases in the costs of materials, fuel services or marketing costs per unit of output;

(3) there are unavoidable increases in capital costs per unit of output; and unless in each of these three cases there are no off-setting reductions either in labour, capital, or non-capital costs per unit of output, or on the return sought on investment; or

(4) after every effort to reduce costs the enterprise is unable to secure the capital required to meet home and overseas demand.

Enterprises will be expected to reduce their prices if:

(1) output is increasing faster than the rate of increase in wages and salaries which is consistent with the criteria for incomes;

(2) costs of materials, fuel or services per unit of output are falling;

(3) capital costs per unit of output are falling, and unless in each of these three cases there are no offsetting and unavoidable increases in other costs per unit of output; or

M

(4) if profits are based on excessive market power.

INCOMES:

Over the 12 months beginning 1st July 1967, no one is entitled to a minimum increase—i.e. the norm is nil—and every increase has to be justified by the following criteria:

(1) where the employees concerned by accepting, for example, more exacting work or a major change in working practices, make a direct contribution to increasing productivity; even in such cases some of the benefit should accrue to the community as a whole in the form of lower prices;

(2) where it is essential in the national interest to secure a change in the distribution of manpower (or prevent a change which would otherwise take place) and to pay increases would be both necessary and effective for this purpose;

(3) where there is a general recognition that existing wage and salary levels are too low to maintain a reasonable standard of living; and

(4) where there is widespread recognition that the pay of a certain group of workers has fallen seriously out of line with the level of remuneration for similar work and needs to be improved in the national interest.

APPENDIX VII

Prices and Incomes Board

The First Forty-two Reports

Index

Index

Index

For Product Safety Concerns and Information please contact our
EU representative GPSR@taylorandfrancis.com Taylor & Francis
Verlag GmbH, Kaufingerstraße 24, 80331 München, Germany